CYCLOPS
IN THE JUNGLE

The Stackpole Military History Series

CYCLOPS IN THE JUNGLE

A One-Eyed LRP in Vietnam

**Staff Sergeant
David P. Walker, USA (Ret.)**

STACKPOLE
BOOKS

Hulen Boyd Horn (1948–2008)
. . . you are missed.

Published by
STACKPOLE BOOKS
5067 Ritter Road
Mechanicsburg, PA 17055
www.stackpolebooks.com

Cover design by Tracy Patterson

Printed in the United States of America

10 9 8 7 6 5 4 3 2 1

Library of Congress Cataloging-in-Publication Data

Walker, David P., 1948–
 Cyclops in the jungle : a one-eyed LRP in Vietnam / by David P. Walker. — 1st ed.
  p. cm. — (Stackpole military history series)
 Includes index.
 ISBN 978-0-8117-3492-9
 1. Vietnam War, 1961–1975—Personal narratives, American. 2. Walker, David P., 1948– I. Title.
 DS559.5.W32 2008
 959.704'342092—dc22
                                   2008003162

*This book is dedicated to the fine men and women,
past, present, and future, who have answered and will answer
our country's call to arms, and especially the members of
Special Operations forces, our fearless helicopter pilots
and their crews, and the combat medics, doctors, and nurses
who retrieved many of us from the precipice of doom.*

*I'd be unforgivably remiss in excluding my faithful wife, Chris;
my daughter, Allison; my grandson, Kenneth IV,
and granddaughters, Isabella and Fayth;
my brother, Gary and his family; my stepson, Jeff;
my wolf puppies, Teva and Skippy; and my kitty, Molly.*

*Dad and Mom, this book is from your son "Wiz,"
and was especially written for you both
to enjoy reading in Heaven.*

Contents

Foreword by Gary A. Linderer

During the three decades since the end of the Vietnam War, hundreds of biographies have been published relating to the individual experiences of the men and women who fought it. Some were poorly written accounts, while others were literary masterpieces. *Cyclops in the Jungle* shares company with the latter.

After every war, there are those who are able to overcome the natural inhibition of warriors to talk about their experiences. It's not an easy thing to do—opening your soul for all to view, revealing the good, the bad, and the ugly. It is so much easier to bury it in the dark spaces where it can't resurface to remind you how close you once came to losing your humanity and, indeed, life itself. However, interment doesn't work with bad memories. Just when you think you've beaten this thing that soaks your sheets and wakes you trembling in the middle of the night, it rises up again and slaps you across the face.

Dave "Varmint" Walker is my brother. He is a fellow F/58th LRP, although our paths never crossed in the service. He lost an eye with the company just six months before I arrived in country. But I knew many LRPs just like Dave. Aggressive, foolishly courageous young men, weighed down with enough piss and vinegar to take on an entire NVA regiment; battle-hardened, jungle-wise, full of machismo and bravado, yet still barely removed from teenaged innocence. Yeah, I knew a lot of young men just like Dave Walker, but he's the only one I know who was medically discharged after a disabling wound, then turned around and maneuvered his way back into the service to do it all again.

Like most of us, Dave was a product of the World War II generation who raised their kids to believe that honoring the flag and serving your country was not only an obligation, but a rite of passage into manhood. We couldn't wait to get out of school and join up. And when we did, most of us picked the infantry for its glory, and a few of us the airborne for its fame, because we had to prove that we were as good as our dads before us. We rushed to the call of the bugle, fearful lest "our" war end before we had a chance to get over there. The day of reckoning arrived sooner than we expected, and we found ourselves stepping off someone else's Freedom Bird into the hot, steamy hell-hole of Vietnam.

It took a special warrior to venture off into no-man's-land with three to six companions. You had to believe that no matter what happened out there, your buddies would never leave you behind. It was the motto of our breed, and we all swore an oath to ourselves never to violate that trust. Dying wasn't so bad when it was for your teammates.

Now, nearly forty years after we slipped silently through the Central Highland triple-canopy jungles of Southeast Asia in pursuit of the enemy, we gather yearly to share a week together. It's not to boast or prove that we are still the men we once were. Rather, we come together to honor the brotherhood and enjoy the camaraderie that only men who have faced a deadly foe and emerged victorious can share. But we also meet to honor those we lost, for they are always with us. Our own time grows shorter until we join them once again for the "eternal mission." Every year a few more names are added to our roster of fallen warriors. Perhaps they are the lucky ones!

Gary A. Linderer
LRP/Ranger, Vietnam

Preface by Roger B. Brown

During my twenty-plus years of enlisted and commissioned active military service with U.S. Army Airborne and Ranger units, many colorful individuals crossed my path. A memorable example is David P. "Varmint" Walker, with whom I first became acquainted in October of 1967 at Fort Campbell, Kentucky. As a staff sergeant cadre member and senior principal instructor for the 101st Airborne Division Recondo School, I was tasked with the responsibility of training and evaluating candidates for the newly forming and Vietnam-bound Division Long Range Patrol Company, and Dave became one of among my twelve carefully selected final class graduates.

We shipped out for Vietnam on December 3, 1967, and a month and a day later, I was tossing Dave on a dustoff helicopter with a serious 82-millimeter mortar shrapnel wound to the left eye. The company soon afterward became engaged in a major combat operation in the Song Be area, and the last word on Dave was that he'd soon be medically evacuated to Japan and eventually stateside with the probability of losing the eye.

Fast forward to early November of 1970 and LZ English (Bong Son), Vietnam. By this time, I was a third-combat-tour sergeant-first-class platoon sergeant with Company N (Ranger), 75th Infantry, attached to the 173rd Airborne Brigade, and had just received a phone call from an old acquaintance, Sgt. John Fowler. Did I know a one-eyed individual named Dave Walker who'd served in F/58 LRP? Totally blindsided, I advised him that yes, I did in fact know Dave. Why was he asking? "He's here with me in Cam Ranh Bay and en route to your rear area at Cha Rang Valley." Thinking fast, I called our company recruiter at Cha Rang, Sgt. C. J. Johnson, and instructed him to drag Dave bag and baggage up to English. If he had the wherewithal and balls to come back here, I'd give him another shot at the big time. In the end run, it was a triple-win deal for Dave, the United States Army, and N/75 Ranger as far as I was concerned.

Dave drove on to serve twenty additional months in-country with N/75 Ranger and a recon platoon in the 196th Light Infantry Brigade. Varmint was one of whom I refer to as my successful LRP/Ranger end products, and I therefore take great pleasure and pride in introducing his Vietnam combat biography.

Capt. Roger B. "Hog" Brown,
USA (Ret.)
LRRP-LRP-Ranger, Vietnam
U.S. Army Ranger Hall of
Fame Inductee

CHAPTER 1

Enlistment and Basic Combat Training

My younger brother, Gary, rendered the "international salute" as I boarded the Greyhound bus from Stockton, California, to Oakland on July 12, 1965. Meanwhile, Dad and Mom both bawled like babies at feeding time. Except for occasional weekend scouting functions and overnight visits with relatives or school friends, this was to be my first solo flight out of the comfort and security of the family roost and, more significantly, would forever define my last day of civilian life. I was embarking upon a journey which, over the next eleven and a half years, would entail several trips around the world and provide me with a first-rate education in real-life coping and survival skills. At the young and impressionable age of seventeen, I was enlisting in the U.S. Army as a volunteer for the infantry and airborne.

Oakland's Greyhound station was located in the seediest section of town. Being a streetwise man, Dad had repeatedly cautioned during the preceding days that Oakland's inhabitants would not have my best interests at heart. Frankly, I was petrified.

In its generosity, the army had reserved a room for me at the world-renowned St. Mark Hotel, located on equally dilapidated San Pablo Avenue. During the short hike from the Greyhound terminal, I must have imagined a mugger lurking in every alleyway or waiting to pounce around the next corner. Abundant along the route were streetwalkers, drunken derelicts, panhandlers, and "professional" ladies with bleach-blonde hair, inch-long false eyelashes, and propositions. Paralyzed with fear, I weakly sputtered a polite refusal. They cackled like witches as I hastily retreated.

The elderly hotel desk clerk teamed me up in a room on the hotel's eighth floor with an eighteen-year-old kid from Sacramento named Jimmy Micek, with whom I'd sweat out the reporting-time vigil of 0800 hours the next morning at the nearby U.S. Armed Forces Entrance and Examining Station (AFEES) on Grand Avenue. Jimmy had been declined for enlistment by the U.S. Navy on a previous occasion because of severe facial acne, and this was his final shot.

We conducted a thorough recon of the most expedient routes for exiting this potential conflagration and funeral pyre, decades overdue for spontaneous combustion. The rickety condition of the fire escape and elevators—not to mention the absence of a TV—immediately confirmed our suspicions that the military hadn't put us up in the Waldorf-Astoria.

The following day, we arose at the desk clerk's zero-dark-thirty wakeup call, and with meal tickets provided by our recruiters in hand, we wearily proceeded to Mel's Drive-In Restaurant for breakfast. Immediately evident, even to neophytes such as us, was Mel's dual mission not only as an eatery, but also a rallying point for prostitutes and their pimps. Despite this mixed company, we were starved and ate like Donner Party cannibals.

Reluctantly arriving at the AFEES, we assumed our places in a long file of enlistees and draftees. The prevailing mood likely matched that of the Bataan Death March. A small group of guys was discussing methods for failing the induction physical, thus achieving draft category 4-F (physical or mental ineligibility). "Just jump off a chair and land heels first! You'll have fallen arches!"

From early to late morning, we completed endless forms and questionnaires. The physical exam seemed to last forever, with the medics prodding us like cattle along color-coded assembly lines and seemingly endless delays between stations. Hurry up and wait!

During the psychological interview, an army medical corps captain inquired about whether I'd ever abused animals, committed arson, attempted suicide, or been physically attracted to other boys, to which I truthfully (scout's honor!) answered "No." Excluding family hardship, sole-surviving-son status, or certifiably disqualifying medical and mental conditions, the gospel word was that the only sure-fire ticket back home was to declare oneself a homosexual.

Miraculously, I met all the exam criteria, and my new medical records jacket was stamped "PHYSICALLY AND MENTALLY QUALIFIED FOR MILITARY SERVICE." Immediately prior to the swearing-in ceremony, we were provided a final opportunity to decline enlistment. Considering the total culture shock and fear I'd experienced since leaving home, I was damned near tempted to jump back on a Greyhound for home. Then the realization struck that I'd never be able to live it down with family and friends, forever being labeled a quitter and, worst of all, a coward.

An Air Force captain administered the oath of enlistment to our group in the late morning. I was now a private basic E-1, Regular Army. The transformation from a carefree high-school kid on summer break to soldier had taken all of about sixty seconds. I was prouder than hell, but still scared out of my wits.

Shortly following the swearing-in ceremony, I was provided a final opportunity to waive my enlistment options for Infantry II and Airborne I training. I'd scored well on the Armed Forces Qualification Test, and I was now told that I could train in the military occupational specialty of my choice, including missiles or electronics. I politely, but firmly, declined. The classification sergeant warned: "David, I hope that you don't regret this farther down the road."

FORT ORD, CALIFORNIA, JULY TO SEPTEMBER 1965

The chartered Peerless Stages bus rolled into the Reception Station at the U.S. Army Training Center, Infantry, Fort Ord, California, at approximately 2230 hours. The false bravado we'd shared and so dearly clung to abruptly waned with the opening of the bus's door. For it was at that fateful moment that Sergeant Burton, our assistant drill instructor, "introduced" himself. "Cat-dogs"—Burtonese for "goddamn"—"you girls have five seconds to un-ass this cat-doggin' bus and plant your feet on the painted white footprints on my company street! The last one of you to do so will be doing pushups until I get tired, and I never get tired, cat-dogs!"

Sergeant Burton herded our exhausted and terrified horde into an overcrowded and overheated classroom, all the while hollering, threatening, and making negative references to our lineages and sexual preferences. Standing before a small podium, he launched into a tirade about filling out forms and sending postcards to our families confirming our safe arrival. "You girls belong to me now, and today was the last day of your lives that you will walk anywhere, cat-dogs! For all of you, the 'block' [civilian life] is already ancient history, and when I tell you to move, you're gonna move, cat-dogs!"

We were issued bedding and awkwardly marched to a two-story wooden barracks in an area of the reception station aptly referred to as "Splinter Village." These buildings had been constructed during World War II and had supposedly been condemned for years.

Staff Sergeant Vibbard, our platoon sergeant and drill instructor, cheerfully greeted our ragtag crew at the barracks, informing us that we were now known as the 5th Platoon. He was a powerfully built Oklahoman who proclaimed his favorite pastime to be double-timing trainees to death on Fort Ord's sandy hills. He patiently instructed us in the army's method of making a bunk with hospital corners and where on the floor to align our soon-to-be-history P.F. Flyers and U.S. Keds. We finally had lights-out at around 0130. My last waking thought was that the new olive-drab wool blanket smelled like mothballs.

The 5th Platoon was rudely awakened ("first call") at 0415, with Staff Sergeant Vibbard enthusiastically yelling obscenities and clanging the fire triangle at the platoon bay's entrance. Sergeant Burton meanwhile flipped on the lights and literally kicked us out of our bunks, screaming, "Off your asses and on your feet, you maggots! I killed all of your mothers last night, and I'm your mother now, cat-dogs!"

The next five days, known as "Zero Week," were devoted to receiving inoculations, drawing uniforms and equipment, learning elementary drill commands, and, of course, receiving the obligatory army "whitewall" haircut. The black-and-white mug shot on my new ID card could just as well have passed for a reform-school inmate.

On July 17, the 5th Platoon relocated "up the hill" into three-story, mid-1950s-vintage concrete barracks known as "New Division," where we were assigned to Headquarters and Headquarters Company, 1st Battalion, 3rd Basic Combat Training Brigade, also known as H-1-3. The training cycle commenced with our acquiring basic military skills and knowledge, i.e., foot and wall locker displays, spit-shining low quarters (dress oxfords) and boots, learning the eleven general orders and the code of conduct, and performing physical training. We memorized the military's phonetic alphabet and learned the twenty-four-hour system for determining local and "Zulu" times.

The army had an obsession for keeping everything neat and tidy, and so existed another revered fatigue duty (manual labor, in other words) known as the "GI party" and its accompanying "white glove inspection." This entailed a microscopic floor-to-ceiling cleanup of our entire living areas, and we spent many an hour on hands and knees scrubbing floor tiles with a toothbrush and scouring powder or stripping old paste wax with a razor blade. If the inspecting officer or NCO found anything less than squeaky clean, we'd have to do the whole thing over again. Although officially forbidden (and unofficially sanctioned), another procedure for living area cleanup, known as the "blanket party," existed for those soldiers disinclined to observe personal hygiene.

Ever since I first saw one on the early-Sixties TV series *The Lieutenant*, I'd eagerly anticipated getting my hands on the M-14 rifle. As a youngster, I'd made the normal transitions from a Daisy Red Ryder BB gun to a Winchester .22 LR five-round bolt-action rifle. Being a fairly good marksman, I incorrectly assumed that the M-14 would also be a piece of cake—my never having fired a high-powered rifle notwithstanding. During the first live "train-fire" session on the beach ranges, the harsh recoil and deafening report of the weapon were unexpected and gave me only ringing ears, a bleeding upper lip, and a bruised shoulder. Honestly, the thing had flat-out intimidated me. Staff Sergeant Buenrostro, our range-safety NCO, scornfully reprimanded me, reinforcing my frustration and misery. When he left my foxhole, I cried my eyes out. I eventually pulled it together and managed to score sixty-three out of seventy points on the final "record fire," qualifing me as "expert."

Within every group of young military trainees, there's always the older prior-service "retread" who acts as a father figure. The 5th Platoon was fortunate to have Melvin Rose, a Korean War vet in his early forties and an oil field worker with Okie roots. A nineteen-year-old old draftee and airborne volunteer platoon mate had been experiencing inordinate emotional hardship adjusting to the army's rigors, and Melvin provided him some "old army" wisdom. "Life in this here man's army gits lots easier when ya finally figger out yer bein' groomed ta be an animal, an' start actin' like one." This rustic but meaningful advice set our newly born-again malcontent on the straight and narrow, further spurring on us other babes-in-arms who might endure a dark day.

Hand-to-hand combat and bayonet drill are skills vital to a soldier's battlefield survival, and we were provided with what proved to be only rudimentary instruction in parries and jabs, pivot kicks, rear takedown and strangle holds, and hip throws. A real-life opponent probably wouldn't stand politely still as the other attempted to inflict bodily harm upon him. I recalled an old axiom Dad had passed on to my brother and me years before: "Never bring a fist to a knife fight, and never bring a knife to a gun fight."

The army steadfastly believed in movies as a training tool, and we endured endless World War II and early-Fifties black-and-white films on venereal disease, personal hygiene, drug abuse, the consequences of going AWOL, enemy spies, you name it. The films also provided an excellent opportunity to catch up on sleep in the overheated theater . . . that is, until the ever-present drill instructor snatched his nocturnal victim by the collar, rudely jerking him into a standing position.

Lengthy road marches with full field pack and combat equipment were a fact of life, and we routinely participated in a marching game known as "GI dominoes." A soldier would stumble on an obstacle—such as a pothole, rock, or deadfall—and do a face-first swan dive to the ground. A chain reaction then usually brought down the soldiers to the first victim's rear, especially at night.

My family paid me a weekend visit, and as she did when I departed Stockton, Mom was again crying. Dad beamed with pride, and Gary was simply awestruck. When Sergeant Burton suggested that I allow Gary to handle my M-14, I knew that I had him hooked. Dad committed a minor breach of protocol by asking Sergeant Burton how I was doing. With a wink, he whispered, "Okay." Sergeant Vibbard feigned disagreement with Sergeant Burton, and Dad was unable to contain a laugh, as were both of my sergeants. In the meantime, I'd been praying that I wouldn't catch hell when my folks left. (I didn't.)

The last stages of training centered on rounding off rough edges and completing required tests. Before we knew it, graduation day was upon us. Only two in our platoon failed to march in the graduation parade. My family again appeared for the ceremonies, as did my old high-school buddy and quasi-adopted brother, Boyd Horn. Dad still beamed with pride, and Mom bawled as usual, while Gary and Boyd acted like what they were: kids (as if I still wasn't one myself).

CHAPTER 2

Advanced Individual Training and Jump School

I departed Fort Ord with permanent change-of-station orders for the U.S. Army Infantry/Military Police School at Fort Gordon, Georgia, for advanced individual training. I arrived after a ten-day leave, which I spent with my family, and was assigned to Company E, 7th Battalion (Airborne Infantry AIT), 3rd Training Brigade.

Obvious to all of us from the beginning of this phase was the relative lack of harassment compared to what we had endured in basic combat training. Every company trainee was an airborne volunteer, and the course centered on the attainment of vital skills and higher standards of discipline that we'd need later not only in an airborne unit, but also in Vietnam. We were still yelled at, but at this stage, it usually served as a reinforcement tool, rather than simply to harass, humiliate, or punish.

The airborne physical-training test was a hurdle we all had to surmount, and the cadre wasted no time implementing a grueling morning PT schedule, hilariously performed to a scratched 33-rpm LP record of the instrumental "Up on the Roof." We ran a minimum of five miles every weekday morning, rain or shine, chanting gung-ho lyrics like "Two old ladies were laying in bed, one rolled over to the other and said, 'I want to be an Airborne Ranger; I want to go to Vietnam; I want to live a life of danger; I want to kill some Charlie Cong!'"

Our company commander, Captain Abraham, insisted on realistic hand-to-hand combat training, and to facilitate this, he'd constructed a replica of the Fort Benning Ranger

Department's Bear Pit. This was basically king of the hill played in reverse, the idea being to eject about twenty opponents from a six-foot-deep pit, leaving yourself as the sole occupant. Captain Abraham had no qualms about our employing dirty tricks or even full contact. "Winners live while losers push up daisies in cemeteries!" he repeatedly emphasized. My 160-pound frame was usually somewhere in the last third to get tossed, while the 190-pound bruisers were almost always the victors. Captain Abraham's version of hand-to-hand training certainly had no parallel with the touchy-feely stuff I'd received in basic combat training.

Infantry advanced individual training maintained the M-14 rifle as the standard shoulder arm, but heavy emphasis was placed on other weapons, such as antipersonnel and antitank weapons. We fired the M-20 3.5-inch rocket launcher, an antitank weapon erroneously referred to by laymen as a "bazooka" (the actual bazooka was the 2.36-inch rocket launcher, years removed from the inventory); the M-18A1 Claymore mine; and the 40-millimeter M-79 grenade launcher (also known as "blooper," "thump-gun," or "thumper"). The Claymore was an especially vicious offensive-defensive weapon. With 1.5 pounds of Composition 4 (C-4) and approximately 800 00-buck steel BBs embedded within its fiberglass-resin case, its fan of effectiveness reached out and touched the enemy to a 100-meter clear area range. The M-79 was also neat, with high-explosive, white-phosphorous ("Willie Pete"), CS (tear gas), star-cluster, a really devastating 00-buck shotgun, and equally nasty canister (dart/flechette) rounds. Its only shortcoming was its 35-meter in-flight arming distance for the high-explosive round—a real problem in thick jungle rain forest. A Special Forces representative from Fort Bragg, North Carolina, demonstrated the M-16 rifle, which to most of us looked like a toy.

We also trained with the M-60 7.62-millimeter light machine gun (nicknamed "pig") and the M-1911A1 .45-caliber pistol. I qualified as an expert with both weapons.

Knowledge of communications was a must, and intensive instruction was provided in radio phraseology and in the maintenance and operation of the AN/PRC-25 FM field radio, AN/PRC-7 (formerly SCR-536) walkie-talkie, and TA-312 field telephone. Directly related to combat communications and intelligence was the SALUTE report (size, activity, location, unit, time, and equipment) for the enemy's status.

Vital for an infantryman is the ability to use a map and compass. Unlike the hasty glossing over we received in basic, we spent many hours in the classroom studying the 1:25,000- and 1:50,000-scale military maps, protractor, and M-3 Lensatic Compass. We learned the use of a "pace cord" as a cumulative distance memory aid—just tie a knot to record distance covered based on a given number of standard thirty-foot strides. Raising our land-navigation training a notch higher, Captain Abraham personally instructed us in the "sun-shadow-stick" and "sun-analog watch" methods of time and direction determination. Initiation and adjustment of indirect fire (naval gunfire, artillery, and mortars) and air strikes went hand-in-hand with map reading. The classroom instruction was followed up with day and night field orienteering courses.

A major training highlight was the escape-and-evasion course. We were paired off into two-man teams, and in the middle of the night, we forded swamps, crashed through thick bramble, and otherwise did all we could to avoid capture by the "aggressors." Dave Edson and I had been partnered up, and although we passed within earshot of the mock prisoner-of-war compound, the aggressors struck out in capturing us. Those less fortunate were subjected to heavy verbal and moderate physical abuse by professional interrogators from the post's military intelligence detachment. Dave and I were overjoyed at not being nabbed, and for the next few days, all of the POWs received endless ribbing.

Camp Crockett was an out-in-the-middle-of-nowhere auxiliary training area of Fort Gordon, and its mock Vietnamese village—complete with "villagers," booby-traps, and "Viet Cong"—was a refreshing change. Master Sergeant Swilly ("The Deacon"), the NCO-in-charge, conducted his classes with a humorously religious flair. When one of us committed the unforgivable sin of getting himself "killed," The Deacon would order the errant soldier to his knees and recite medieval gibberish, the meaning of which only he understood. He then blessed the newly departed soul with his "mystical scepter," a GI bunk adapter with costume jewels cemented to the shaft and an authentically carved and painted wooden penis and testicles secured to the end.

Since the cycle had begun, we'd been preparing for two primary objectives. A pass or fail on the Infantry Skill Level One Proficiency Test determined graduation, recycling, or transfer to another training course. The maximum score attainable was 185, hence our motto, "Airborne, can do 185!" And successful negotiation of the airborne physical-training test was compulsory for shipment to the Fort Benning Airborne School. Captain Abraham and the cadre had been unyielding taskmasters, and virtually the entire class aced both tests.

We graduated as qualified and proud light-weapons infantrymen ("11B for you and me!") on Friday, December 2, 1965, and bade farewell to Fort Gordon, bound for jump school.

JUMP SCHOOL

As the chartered Trailways bus approached Fort Benning's Eubanks Field from the Lumpkin Road gate, everyone onboard gazed wide-eyed at the red aircraft obstruction lights outlining the ghostly shadows of the 250-foot free-training towers. Reportedly, the towers had been erected in 1940 by the same engineering firm that had designed the Chute ride at Coney Island.

We had heard all kinds of rumors about the greeting we'd get at the airborne reception center, and the mystery was resolved when two black-hatted airborne instructors stormed onto the bus, forcibly extricated the drive, and then kicked and screamed us into a four-rank formation outside the bus. They rudely ordered us into the pushup position, one black hat commanding, "And I'd better-by-God not see a belly touch my dear, darling Fort Benning, goddamnit!" This was followed by the "duck walk," a form of harassment made no easier by the seventy-five-pound duffle bags we were carrying. We lost at least three people through these terror tactics, and we hadn't even been on Fort Benning for an hour.

We were packed into a small auditorium and issued roster numbers. I drew 779 and was assigned to the 48th Company, 4th Battalion, The Student Brigade, Class 21, with the balance of my advanced individual training class. In a one-in-a-million chance of fate, two of my Manteca High associates, Charlie Luxner and John Fonseca, were present. The three of us agreed on the spot that mutual support from homeboys was priceless under the circumstances.

Having arrived on a Friday night, our only immediate concerns were dodging weekend details (like KP) and eluding the cadre (especially black hats). Naturally, we'd all long since deluded ourselves into believing that we had mastered the time-honored military skill known as "ghosting." To illustrate this point, Gus Higdon hid in his wall locker during the manhunt for KPs early Saturday morning. Poor Gus spent the entire weekend on KP.

Monday morning began at zero-dark-thirty with a vengeance. We were fallen out onto the company street and placed into the "dying cockroach" position (on the back, with head, arms and legs off the ground—very painful), duck-walked, and given countless pushups. The black hats conducted yet another grueling physical-trianing session and run, after which we were finally double-timed to breakfast.

At Eubanks Field, we received a formal welcome from Col. Bill Welch, an airborne legend. He emphasized the hazards inherent in military parachute jumping and candidly informed us that serious injuries or fatalities, although not the norm, were distinct factors to consider.

A briefing on what would take place over the next three-week period followed. Week one (Ground Week) would focus on our mastery of front, rear, and side parachute landing falls;

equipment familiarization; mock-door, suspended-harness ("suspended agony" or "nutcracker") drag recovery using a vehicle-mounted wind machine; and swing-landing parachute landing fall (PLF) training. Tower Week concentrated on applying the skills we'd attained during Ground Week on the thirty-four-foot procedures and 250-foot free-training towers. Week three, not surprisingly known as Jump Week, would separate the men from the boys, we were told, as the previous two weeks would culminate in five parachute jumps on Fryar Drop Zone in Alabama.

Since the beginning of Jump Week, the instructors had repeatedly hammered home that any student observed executing a "stand-up" landing, which could be very dangerous when misjudged, would—at the very least—receive an Article 15 (non-judicial punishment) and fail the course. Any injury would be considered "not in the line of duty," and the individual would be subject to possible court-martial under the "Failure to Repair" statute. Hilariously, to wantonly or negligently injure or kill oneself in the military constitutes "defacing and/or destruction of government property." Naturally, along with most of my classmates, I vowed to try one on the graduation jump.

Jump Week finally arrived, and the harassment we'd endured over the preceding two weeks abruptly ceased. Our first four jumps would be executed in non-combat-equipment ("Hollywood") configuration from Lockheed C-130 Hercules aircraft. Additionally, each jumper would perform an individual exit ("tap out").

The class was marched to the nearby Lawson Army Airfield launch point. In sincere attempts to allay our doubts and fears, the instructors jested that on this fine, lovely morning, we'd all be taking a one-way airplane trip to Alabama. The catch was that although we'd be landing there, the aircraft wouldn't. As a final measure to quell our apprehensions, they tongue-in-cheekily reminded us that night jumps were not included in the basic airborne training syllabus. Therefore, we were to keep our eyes open at all times during the jump.

The short flight to Fryar at 1,250 feet above ground level was nauseating for many of us. The C-130, like most military transport aircraft, has few fuselage windows, and the lack of outside orientation, combined with heat and emotional stress, can induce vertigo and airsickness in even lightly turbulent air. In hopes of preventing accidents with the associated cleanup, the air force loadmasters provided us with barf bags. Several students aboard our aircraft lost their lunch, and the reek permeated the cabin, creating in turn a limited chain reaction. The loadmasters instructed these unfortunates to seal the bags and exit with them.

The jumpmasters' opening of the left (port) and right (starboard) troop exit doors came as a rude shock to all of us. The slipstream and the four Allison turbo shaft prop-jet engines weren't only deafening, but overwhelming. It was totally unlike anything most of us had ever experienced and could best be compared to the roar of a titanic blast furnace in a steel mill. The C-130 carried sixty-four students, equally divided into two rows on each side of the aircraft, known as "sticks." Since I occupied the number one (rear), or "stick leader," position in the second stick on the port inboard side of the aircraft, I'd have the opportunity to observe sixteen jumpers precede me.

The left door jumpmaster issued the first six of the eight jump commands: "Get ready! Outboard personnel, stand up! Hook-up! Check static lines! Check equipment! Sound off for equipment check!" The last two commands—"Stand in the door!" and "Go!"—would be issued during each "tap-out."

Having witnessed three jump refusals from the first stick, my number finally came up. I felt the jumpmaster's obligatory smack on my butt and made a piss-poor exit (I was petrified!) into the violent 125-knot slipstream. The main parachute backpack struck the fuselage just aft of the troop exit door a light glancing blow, and I remember being momentarily inverted and watching the floodlit cabin interior rapidly decrease in size.

As abruptly as the chaos had begun, it ceased in the blink of an eye. All was relatively silent, save the departing C-130's ominous drone, and I was floating in space. The opening shock hadn't nearly matched the horror stories promoted by the black hats. Finally gathering my wits, I ecstatically realized that any challenging amusement park rides I'd conquered in civilian life paled in comparison to the one I'd just taken.

As per training, I checked canopy and was greeted with beautifully blossomed main panels, but moderately twisted suspension lines and risers, a consequence of my collision with the aircraft. I was in a slowly unwinding right rotation and began a bicycle maneuver combined with hand-spreading the risers to straighten things out. Undoubtedly stemming from the adrenaline rush and disbelief of having survived, we first-time jumpers waved and yelled to one another, experiencing an elation known only to those who've been there. Instructors on the ground meanwhile chided us through bullhorns to slip into the wind, keep our feet and knees together, knees slightly bent, eyes locked on the horizon to avert anticipation of impact, and hit-shift-rotate in a proper direction upon landing.

I struck the hard-packed red Alabama clay on Fryar Drop Zone like a ton of bricks, executing a perfect two-point rear parachute landing fall (the balls of my feet and the backside of my helmet). Luckily, the drop zone safety officer hadn't observed my substandard—and dangerous—landing. Four jumps to go!

The day's jump-refusals were expelled from our midst to holding-company purgatory as though they were plague-ridden. These unfortunate washouts would languish in nonstop shit details while awaiting orders to non-airborne "leg" (lacking enough guts to jump) units in Vietnam. The majority of us hadn't chickened out, and we boldly swapped tales of our natural aptitude for jumping late into the evening. An advanced individual training classmate, Tommy Gaylord, had witnessed my exiting impact with the aircraft, and I was thereafter tagged as "Ricochet."

Units of assignment were soon posted, and I drew the 82nd Airborne Division ("All American"), based at Fort Bragg, North Carolina. Even though we hadn't quite finished jump school, along with my classmates, I took the calculated risk of rushing to the alterations shop to have jump wings and unit patches sewn on my uniforms.

We were out of our racks well before first call on Friday morning. This was the big day, and the excitement over having our wings almost within reach was evident in everyone. If events went as planned, I'd depart Fort Benning the following evening as an airborne-qualified PV2 in the U.S. Army, with my newest paycheck reflecting the associated $55.00 hazardous duty pay. If not, I'd be shipped home in a U.S. Government casket tagged "Unsuitable for Viewing."

The graduation jump included full combat equipment, which added about eighty pounds to the jumper's weight—and many more chances for a SNAFU. Hell, just donning the extra stuff and boarding the aircraft was an exhausting chore.

Struggling to the troop exit door, heavily burdened with all the gear, including an M-14 strapped to the harness, I literally fell out of the aircraft. At an estimated altitude of 400 feet, I yanked the red "lollipop" knob to release the parachutist airborne equipment bag on its shock cord lowering strap. At around forty or fifty feet, I pulled a four-riser slip until reaching about ten feet and released the risers. My boots struck the ground as if I'd been lightly set down on a bed of cotton, and I just stood there, not quite believing what I'd just done. Miraculously, I'd once again escaped the all-seeing eyes of the drop zone safety officer during the stand-up landing, and during the run to the marshalling area, I yelled out of sheer joy while watching fellow students earn their wings.

With all new graduates reassembled, Colonel Welch addressed the formation, welcoming Class 21 into the airborne fraternity. He stated that from this day on, we'd never again be just average men, but rather members of a very elite corps. He concluded his address with a solemn admonition: "Never bring discredit upon your uniform, your unit, or the wings that you're about to receive." In unison, our entire class bellowed: "Clear sir! . . . Airborne! . . . Class 21! . . . Fight forever! . . . Quit never!"

Like every man, friend or foe, who has graduated from a military parachutist training course, I'll never forget the actual moment of receiving my wings. Sergeant First Class Alston took one step from the man on my right and executed a left face. He pinned on my wings, shook my hand, and in an almost fatherly manner said, "Congratulations, young paratrooper!" I'll never be able to put into words the intense exhilaration and boundless pride I felt at that moment.

CHAPTER 3

Marking Time

82ND AIRBORNE DIVISION, JULY TO AUGUST 1966

I arrived at Fort Bragg, North Carolina, on January 8, 1966. We new arrivals were greeted harshly by 1st Sgt. "Blood" Burns: "All of you goddamned cherry five-jump commandos form a circle and commence duck-walking to my military right, meaning your military left, thus creating a mirror image, *now*!! Welcome, one and all, to *my* 82nd Airborne Division!"

First Sergeant Burns was a hulking, menacing black man well over six feet and 200 pounds (none of it fat). His booming bass voice commanded undivided attention from us so-called cherries. According to the airborne NCO old boy network, Burns routinely drowned cherry KPs in the repo-depot's mess hall grease trap. In reality, he was just your typical grandiose airborne teddy bear senior NCO who loved the army and his troops, especially newly graduated cherries.

On the third day, I was assigned to Company A, 3rd Battalion (Airborne), 325th Infantry. The short jeep ride up Ardennes Road to my new home, although exciting, wasn't without apprehension on my part. En route, the company clerk, PFC John Utley, provided a brief rundown on what the company had recently been doing: unpacking from its recent deployment to the Dominican Republic. John told me that I was being assigned to the 4th Platoon with 2nd Lieutenant Cox and Staff Sergeant McCoy, a veteran of World War II and Korea who wore just about every airborne-infantry badge in existence.

The company returned from a local field training exercise in the early afternoon, and I was reunited with Dave Edson, my advanced individual training and airborne classmate, and

Roger Seyl from my basic combat training platoon. Needless to say, it was good seeing familiar faces in this new and very intimidating environment.

Sergeant McCoy commandeered me the following morning for introductions to 1st Sgt. C. L. Tackel and 1st Lt. Samuel K. O'Neal, the company commander. Top Tackel was also a World War II and Korea veteran, and his snow-white hair made him appear to be in his mid-60s. Lieutenant O'Neal had recently returned from a Military Assistance Command, Vietnam (MACV), advisory assignment and had been seriously wounded by Russian RPG-7 shrapnel to the throat and mouth. With a raspy voice, he welcomed me into the company, solemnly cautioning that I should pay close attention during training.

The physical-training schedule was grueling. The 82nd Airborne maintained a twenty-four-hour worldwide response through its immediate reaction force and division ready force status, and we had to be physically prepared for combat in any climate and environment.

I'd been in the unit for about two weeks when the battalion was alerted for a scheduled night Hollywood jump on Normandy Drop Zone. I was excited as hell. Not only would I be busting my cherry, a subject which we new people hadn't heard the end of up to this point, but it would be at night.

We boarded the C-130s, and the red floodlit cabin interior created a ghostly atmosphere. The absence of color definition caused by the neutral light only served to intensify this effect. I leaped into the pitch-black void amidst a herd of stampeding cattle, and contrary to what I'd anticipated, the experience induced minor disorientation as opposed to fear, which quickly diminished. Despite the darkness, I was able to just barely discern the silhouettes of other jumpers' canopies surrounding me. Other than faint halos of light on the distant horizon, the only visible ground reference was a code letter "T," faintly defined by battery-powered Pathfinder lights.

The jump had been designated as supposedly tactical in nature, and Lieutenant O'Neal had earlier lectured us on the necessity for strict light and noise discipline. In anticipation of the jump, many of us, especially the cherries, had purchased Kodak Instamatic cameras and snapped away while whooping and hollering up and down the drop zone. The most vivid recollection of this, my first night jump, was the totally penetrating damp cold of that January night in North Carolina.

The day after the jump, we newly busted cherries were gathered in the platoon bay for the old airborne initiation rite known as the prop-blast party. We were given some airborne-style liquid refreshment called prop-blast—a lethal concoction of hot sauce, booze, beer, and God-knows-what-else poured into a Corcoran jump boot. Under the close supervision of our seniors, we each guzzled the witch's potion out of an empty boot. Since I up-chucked every drop of the toxic stuff immediately following its consumption, I was spared the debilitating hangover. Nevertheless, I had been properly "blasted."

Our squad leader, SP4 Jim Christopher, whom we called Chris, was a recent 173rd Airborne veteran of Vietnam, and he took our training, health, and welfare seriously, perhaps excessively so. When we'd commit the errors common to inexperienced soldiers, Chris would become enraged, sometimes to the point of physically assaulting the errant individual(s), exclaiming that substandard performance during training would earn us a one-way-ticket home from Vietnam in a body bag.

Along with a promotion to private first class during February 1966 came an additional thirty dollars in pay as well as single gold chevrons for my sleeves. With my eighteenth birthday fast approaching, the promotion also rendered me as prime pickings for the Vietnam levy under the so-called "E-3 and 18" rule for assignment to a combat zone. This fact hadn't in the least eluded Mom, who, having closely monitored the war's progress from Huntley-Brinkley and Walter Cronkite, had started expressing a marked desire for her son's immediate change of military occupational specialty.

The company received word of its first Vietnam combat casualty through the *Army Times*. A sister platoon member, Jerry Crocker, had departed for Vietnam in the last part of January and had been killed in action shortly thereafter while serving with the 1st Brigade, 101st Airborne. Top Tackel and recently promoted Captain O'Neal experienced literal shit fits over the news.

The 82nd Airborne loved to jump, and during the month of May, the battalion participated in two blasts. The first was a daytime Hollywood jump from a Lockheed C-141 Starlifter, and the second was a nighttime, full-combat-equipment operation from the historic twin-boom Fairchild C-119 Flying Boxcar.

Mom's unrelenting pressure for me to seek a safer calling finally won the toss. I recalled the Oakland AFEES processing NCO's attempt to push missile training and decided to go for it.

I soon visited the 2nd Brigade Reenlistment NCO, Staff Sgt. "Goose" Gosselin. The guy could easily have doubled for a used-car salesman or game-show emcee by anyone's standards ("Dave Walker, come on down!"). Goose's interview commenced with the usual query over ACB scores, education level, disciplinary record, and of course, what I wanted to do in the Army. My enthusiastic answer was "Nike missile training close to Manteca, California, sarge—I mean Goose!"

"Good choice, Dave! Missile men live like royalty! Hmm, Nike missile bases near Manteca, California . . . how far is that from San Francisco, Dave?"

"About seventy-five miles or so, Goose."

"Well, I show a place here called Fort Baker in Sausalito, Marin County, and it's administratively attached to the Presidio of San Francisco."

"Big R" day came on July 14. With Lieutenant Cox, Top Tackel, Staff Sergeant McCoy, and Chris in attendance, I was sworn in by our battalion commander, Lieutenant Colonel Doehlman at 3rd Battalion HQ as a private first class in the Regular Army, thus incurring a renewed three-year service commitment.

In typical army fashion, I received orders for the 1st Brigade, 101st Airborne Division, in Vietnam about a week following the re-up ceremony. This placed me in a quandary in that the army presented me with the choice of complying with my pending orders for Fort Baker or going to Vietnam. Either way, I'd be stuck with the re-up obligation.

Mom went critical when I mentioned the Vietnam orders. Was I aware, she blurted, that Brock Elliot had just been killed in Vietnam with the 1st Marine Division? Brock, whom I'd known only casually at Manteca High, hailed from a very prominent Manteca family and had graduated with the class of '65, joining the marines immediatcly afterward. He'd been killed sometime during early 1966, becoming the first of Manteca's total of seventeen Vietnam combat fatalities. Years later, Brock D. Elliot Elementary School would be named in his honor. My reassurance that all remained as planned finally set Mom at ease.

As what I considered to be a suitable departure gift, the battalion was assigned two successive daytime Hollywood jumps on Salerno Drop Zone. We'd be jumping out of California Air National Guard Douglas C-124 Globemasters. The C-124 was a huge and lumbering late-1940s four-engine piston transport with a fuselage that looked like a sardine in need of Slim-Fast. It was phased out of the air force's inventory a short time later, finally overtaken by the C-141, and it was a genuine privilege to have had the opportunity to jump out of such an historical airplane.

After that jump and with some misgivings, I cleared post on August 7 and said my last good-byes to the 4th Platoon and A Company. Ten military parachute jumps wasn't too shabby for a young PFC.

ARMY AIR DEFENSE COMMAND, SEPTEMBER TO NOVEMBER 1966

Reporting to Fort Baker, California, wasn't without its unpleasantries. The desperately grateful reception I'd anticipated from Headquarters and Headquarters Battery, 2nd Battalion, 51st Air Defense Artillery (Nike Hercules), wasn't to be. Sergeant First Class Lopez and I immediately hit it off poorly with my comment—meant as a joke—of having been sentenced to a "leg" unit.

Since I'd arrived just after normal duty hours, PFC Danny Snodgrass ("Grass"), the battery clerk and my next-door neighbor, invited me to the nearby combined "Silo" EM/NCO club to get acquainted over some beers. As the buzz began wearing off, I reflected on just where I'd come up to this point in the army. The inescapable conclusion was that I should have just accepted the orders for Vietnam.

Danny Snodgrass was a genuinely nice kid of twenty from Salem, Oregon, and had joined the Army in October 1965. He was the stereotypical nerd with thick horn-rimmed glasses and dandruff who excelled at dissecting frogs in biology class or operating the classroom movie projector but tripped over himself on the athletic field. I instinctively knew that his choice to be a "Remington Raider" had nothing to do with cowardice. I also instantly liked Danny, and he was fascinated with my having gone to jump school, which suited my presently deflated ego just fine. SP4 Larry Hankins, my other neighbor and a recent 101st Airborne returnee from Vietnam, proved yet another godsend to my morale. At least there was one other guy wearing jump wings in this rathole directly over the San Andreas fault line.

The battery members spent a day at the Fort Baker firing range (a scene from *The Enforcer*, a *Dirty Harry* installment, was filmed there years later). Annual weapons qualification was on the training schedule, and I'd have to once again display my proficiency with the M-1911 service auto *and* the M-2 carbine (an M-1 carbine with selective semi/auto-fire capability), which I'd never even handled before. I maxed the .45, and the M-2 was also a walk in the park, although as far as I was concerned, you couldn't hit a running man-size target beyond about fifty meters—it was a very loose weapon. As for poor Danny, I could barely contain my laughter when he attempted to field-strip the M-1911. The way I remember it, the weapon virtually disintegrated in his hands after he'd turned and released the barrel bushing, the operating spring and its retainer sleeve flying off into the wild blue yonder. His luck with the M-2 wasn't any better, despite my assisting him in establishing his "battle-sight zero."

I'd always wanted to walk across the Golden Gate Bridge just to be able to say I'd done so. On an unusually sunny Friday morning, with Danny and Larry along for company, we hiked the short distance up the Fort Baker access road to the midpoint of the lower north tower. We observed an aircraft carrier approaching from East Bay Alameda Navy Base and had ample time to reach the bridge's mid-span to observe its departure (probably to Yankee Station in the Tonkin Gulf). From our high perch on the pedestrian walkway, the carrier *Enterprise*, identified by the bold "65" on the fore and aft deck as well as the superstructure, passed gracefully beneath us. Numerous deck crewmen exchanged waves and salutes with us, and the superstructure's antenna mast appeared as if about to strike the lower bridge framework. I felt as if I could just reach out and grab an antenna. We all kicked ourselves in the asses for not having brought cameras, but it was a truly unforgettable experience.

The alert for overseas movement arrived in the first part of November. It turned out to be a direct assignment to Company B, 1st Battalion, 509th Infantry (Airborne/Mechanized)—in Germany, for crying out loud! I was infuriated by the news, and all I could conjure up were visions of amputated frostbitten toes and fingers in some godforsaken place like the Black Forest.

All Mom cared about was the 1049 for Vietnam having been a bust. Dad had served with the U.S Office of Strategic Services as a French/German interpreter and interrogator in England until the Normandy invasion, after which he followed the troops across Europe until a German potato-masher grenade earned him a metal kneecap. He attempted to make me see the bright side of the situation, emphasizing the good food and ample supply of women. I diplomatically told Dad that this was all truly outstanding, but since I'd probably be spending all of my time on field training exercises or trying to stay alive during race riots, I'd be in a piss-poor position to take advantage of these perks. Worse yet, the typical European assignment amounted to a thirty-six-month stabilized tour.

The entire situation seemed totally cockeyed to me. Here there were countless individuals, both in and out of the military, employing every trick in the book to avoid service in Vietnam, and all I wanted was simply to get my gung-ho young ass over there to function in the job I'd been trained for.

No sooner were the orders in my hands than I'd cleared post. A fifteen-day delay en route was authorized, with a reporting date of no later than midnight on November 30, 1966, at Fort Dix, New Jersey, for overseas processing.

509TH AIRBORNE/MECHANIZED INFANTRY ("THE FIVE-O-NASTY"), DECEMBER 1966 TO JANUARY 1967

The Fort Dix Overseas Replacement Center turned out to be yet another army peon's hellhole, but I successfully dodged the shit details. We completed processing for overseas replacement on the morning of December 3 and boarded a chartered TWA Boeing 727 at McGuire Air Force Base early in the afternoon. Our MAC boarding passes listed Rhein-Main Air Base near Frankfurt, Germany, as the aircraft's destination.

I cynically envisioned what was in store for me on the other end. Despite the direct assignment, I'd been told that all new Army arrivals in Germany were required to process through the dreaded 21st Replacement Detachment in Frankfurt. According to Fort Dix repo-depot legend, the 21st had been the origin of the nickname "animal farm" for army personnel replacement centers. Hostile racial encounters were routine, and low rankers languished in misery on one shit detail after another while awaiting assignment to their units. Our stay at 21st turned out to be only three hours.

After about an hour on the road, we arrived at Robert E. Lee Barracks, home of the 1st and 2nd Battalions of the 509th Airborne Infantry (Mechanized). Located virtually in the center of downtown, it was a huge complex with endless rows of three-story quadrangles seeming to extend as far as the eye could see. The motor pool was an immense cobblestone affair, packed with line after line of M-113 armored personnel carriers and M-60 tanks.

First Sergeant Hoolapa, affectionately known by all as "Hula-Hoop," assigned me to the 4th Platoon. Since the company was on maneuvers in some strange place named Kaiserslautern, the first sergeant suggested that I get some chow and rest and, in general, get the lay of the land. In what appeared to be genuine concern for my welfare, he strongly urged that I not depart the kaserne alone.

The company commander, Captain Hussong, was a seldom-seen entity, and the NCOs and younger combat veterans pretty much ran the unit's everyday operations. Cpl. Roy Jones, my squad leader, represented the higher caliber of these men. Roy had recently returned from a Vietnam tour with the 173rd Airborne Brigade and would provide me with priceless European and Vietnam survival skills.

With the majority of the new M-16 rifles being allocated to Vietnam, the 509th remained equipped with the M-14. Once again having to verify my marksmanship skills despite the recent qualification at Fort Baker, I scored a max seventy points. The comical part was that rather than the electrically activated pop-up targets, the local range was equipped with the old style manually raised bull's-eye targets, exactly like those from the old *Sergeant York* movie with Gary Cooper.

Roy assigned me to an on-the-job-training gunner slot on the M-67 90-millimeter recoilless rifle, which was just then replacing the 3.5-inch rocket launcher. The weapon weighed about thirty-five pounds empty, with another twelve pounds added for a loaded round and a telescopic sight. It was an ass-kicker to carry in the field, and I prayed that I'd never have to *jump* with the damned thing. Its deafening report was enough to make an unwary bystander jump out of his Corcorans—and don't ever get caught in the backblast! What had long since become obvious to me was that *everything* in the airborne infantry was loud or dangerous—and most often both.

The nightmares I'd envisioned over the hardships endured on European FTXs became reality in short order. The battalion mounted a two-day excursion to a frozen mountainous forest hell called Baumholder. The hours-long en route phase on cobblestone roads in the M-113s was truly luxurious on the thinly padded metal troop seats, and setting up defensive positions in the waist-deep snow and nearly permafrost ground was even more joyous. You've never experienced true misery and frustration until you've attempted to dig a foxhole under such conditions with a GI entrenching tool. No fires were allowed—naturally—and the reason for my having been issued Arctic mittens, parka, and insulated "Mickey Mouse" boots became painfully obvious. Humping the 90-millimeter was totally exhausting, and the only respite came in alternating it with my assistant gunner. As I'd envisioned, the powers-that-be had no objections to operating our M-60 tanks and tracks in close proximity to the troops . . . in total blackout conditions.

Bammm-bammm-bammm!!! Whoooosh!!! Clang!! The harsh explosions shattered all of the platoon bay windows facing our rear company street. Instantly alerted out of a sound sleep, I fearfully said to myself that this was one hell of a way to be awakened for first call. A few of us summoned the nerve to take a peek outside and were greeted with the sight of burning trash in and around the dumpster. The dumpster's steel hatch lay about fifty feet from its proper resting place, and a nearby jeep's radiator was leaking coolant.

The detonations had occurred in near-simultaneous succession, and most of us at first thought their source to be some of the granddaddy-size M-80s or cherry bombs readily available from German street vendors—possibly even artillery simulators. Having had firsthand experience with things of this nature, Roy brought it to our attention that none of the latter would penetrate .125-inch-thick steel. The logical assumption, therefore, was that hand grenades or other military explosives devices such as TNT or C-4 had discharged in the dumpster.

All battalion members were restricted to their company areas while the MPs and Criminal Investigation Division agents conducted a sweep of all living areas. The CIDs, as they were called, wore no rank insignia, instead wearing officer "U.S." devices on their shirt collars and fatigue caps. As Roy put it, you might be dealing with an SP4—or a major.

Strolling into an otherwise vacant platoon bay later that afternoon, I was ominously met by Captain Hussong, First Sergeant Hoolapa, Staff Sergeant Smith, and two CID agents. I immediately observed that my wall locker, foot locker, and laundry bag had been ransacked, and one of the CID agents pointedly asked me: "Walker, where in the hell are the frags?" Caught totally off guard, I almost immediately burst into tears, shakily asking the agent what he was talking about. He responded, "The case of M-26 fragmentation grenades you pilfered during your guard duty tour at the Rudesheim ammo dump the night before last!" Desperately attempting to compose myself, I informed the agent that my guard post assignment had been the ammo dump's entry gate, a stationary position. I hadn't left the post during the tour, and no persons other than the commander of the relief and officer of the guard had entered the compound.

Following an hour or so of grilling by the CID agents and Captain Hussong, I was placed under house arrest pending further investigation. In my terrified state of mind, the only positive aspect of this was that I hadn't been cuffed and hauled off outright to the universally dreaded Mannheim Stockade (wasn't that where they hung people?).

Sergeant First Class Zamski, the company operations NCO, requested my presence in his office that evening. He was known to be a fair type, and despite my still relative naiveté, I figured this to be an interrogation tactic suggested by the CIDs: reduce the subject's defensive posture and vigilance through employment of the old "I'm on your side, and I want to help you" routine, and maybe he'd come to Jesus. Offering me a chair and a cup of coffee, Zamski freely admitted that what he decided during our conversation would have a major bearing on where I'd spend that night and possibly many others.

For the better portion of two hours, I was asked all variety of questions, ranging from my date and place of birth to whether I had ever used fireworks as a kid (I honestly answered that I had). Had I ever engaged in violent activities against others? Well, if one considered routine childhood fights to be wantonly violent engagements, my goose was cooked. Had I ever committed a crime? At the age of seven, my second-grade classmate Steve Oliver invited me to his house for afterschool play. Searching in an overhead kitchen cabinet for munchies, Steve, whose dad was a Southern Pacific Railroad detective, discovered a carelessly placed (and loaded) off-duty .38-cal service revolver. Having successfully begged for Steve to allow me to touch it, I then proceeded to discharge a round into the kitchen wall. My ears rang for what seemed like hours afterward, and neither of us escaped hearing the end of that brilliant stunt for months. It was also one of the few times in my entire life that I'd witnessed Dad literally turn white from shock.

Sergeant First Class Zamski almost broke into a smile as I'd confessed my criminal past. I suppose that my rosy red cheeks and peach-fuzz stubble also helped my case, and he flatly stated that I'd never been seriously considered as a suspect following the initial afternoon contact.

The actual culprits, three Black Power militants from our sister Company A, were apprehended a few days later. They'd cut through the chain link fence with heavy-duty dikes and removed the padlock on a grenade bunker with a bolt cutter. The word was that they'd intended to "frag" a number of officers and NCOs who'd been assembling a drug case on them. All of them received dishonorable discharges and one-way, all-expenses-paid plane trips to Leavenworth.

I made my first jump since departing Fort Bragg three weeks after arriving in-country. It was a nighttime Hollywood C-130 operation on snow-covered Mannheim Drop Zone, and the landing virtually matched in softness that of my graduation jump at Benning. The downside came with the hike back to the marshalling area in knee-deep snow. Well, at least I was drawing jump pay again.

EIGHTH DIVISION AIRBORNE SCHOOL,
JANUARY TO SEPTEMBER 1967

A reprieve from the Five-O-Nasty came totally unexpectedly early on the morning of January 31. Cpl. Dave Serna, a representative from the 8th Infantry Division Airborne School, was on the hunt for a new operations clerk. I'd taken typing during my sophomore year at Manteca High, could type thirty-five (relatively) error-free words per minute, and won the competition against five other hopefuls hands-down. By 0800, I was shuffling joyously out of the barracks, duffle bag in hand, bound for a new life.

Located on nearby Wiesbaden Air Base, the 8th Infantry Division Airborne School, along with its sister 10th SFGA Jump School at Bad Toelz, was one of only two U.S. parachute training centers in the European theater, and Wiesbaden graduates were sometimes unflatteringly referred to as "Wiesbaden Wonders." We were quartered in a modern air-conditioned building, and our neighbors down the hallway were the U.S. Air Force Combat Control Team, all of whom would eventually come to be my close friends.

Capt. Charles L. "Chuck" Presnall was the school commandant, and Sgt. 1st Class Hal Roach was our "sergeant major." Among the school cadre, I was reunited with Master Sgt. Ray Manning and Sgt. 1st Class Randy Glover, both of whom had been my instructors at Fort Benning. It was really outstanding being on the other side of the fence for a change, and I'd even be wearing a black baseball cap, just like the grownups.

Staff Sgt. Richard S. Carmen ran the school operations room and was my immediate supervisor. What instantly struck me was the informality amongst the school cadre. Except for Captain Presnall, of course, everyone dealt with each other on a first-name or even nickname basis, regardless of rank. Sergeant Carmen preferred just Rick, while Staff Sgt. Ellis answered to "Big E" and Sergeant Owens "Big O."

My specific duties were outlined during an initial meeting with Captain Presnall, Sergeant Major Roach, and Rick. I'd be responsible for completion of all training schedules, records, reports, and miscellaneous unit paperwork. When time permitted, I'd serve as an assistant instructor and demonstrator during class presentations. During Rick's absence, I'd in effect be the operations NCO, which Captain Presnall emphasized was a great deal of responsibility for a private first class. Best of all, I'd be entitled to virtually unlimited jumping with the classes and CCT guys, time permitting.

The folks sent word during June that Gary had just enlisted in the army with his junior-high and high-school pal Dave Bulmer under the buddy system. He'd be attending basic combat training at Fort Lewis, Washington, thereafter transferring to Fort Ord, California, for infantry advanced individual training. The word "infantry" immediately activated red lights and klaxons in my head, and of one thing I was adamant: if either one of us was going to buy the farm in Vietnam, it would be me.

Pete Gerspach received orders for the 173rd Airborne in Vietnam and was gone in a flash. The Vietnam levy was still alive and well, as it always had been. Once again, Gary's present status popped into my mind. As for Boyd, he'd written me several times since our separation and was in relatively safe circumstances as a boiler man aboard the USS *Wright*, a signal intelligence (spook) ship.

As a rule, Captain Presnall was a very even-tempered individual, but his dark side evidenced itself early one morning while browsing the European *Stars and Stripes*. I heard him yell, "Sonofabitch!" from the dayroom as he pitched the newspaper to the floor. Captain Presnall's outburst attracted attention from several of us, and when I finally had my turn at seeing what all of the ruckus was about, there, in bold black newsprint, was SP4 Peter J. Gerspach's name listed on the latest Vietnam KIA list.

Pete's loss did it for me right then and there. I typed up a 1049 personnel action for Vietnam that afternoon, reluctantly endorsed by Captain Presnall, specifying the 173rd Airborne as a preferred unit of assignment. An added advantage of being the operations clerk was the freedom to hand-carry the thing to the 8th's headquarters at Bad Kreuznach for final approval. I'd get a few gooks for Pete.

The orders for Vietnam arrived in record time during early September. I was less than overjoyed to discover they indicated assignment to the 101st Airborne at Fort Campbell, Kentucky, for further overseas movement to Vietnam. A fifteen-day delay en route to Campbell was also included, which hopefully would provide me the opportunity to talk some sense into Gary, who by now was at Fort Ord.

I was totally unprepared for Captain Presnall's going-away memento: an obviously expensive shield-shaped plaque with a mounted airborne soldier in full combat equipment. The engraved brushed metal placard below the figurine read: "SP4 David P. Walker . . . Cadre . . . 8th Infantry Division Airborne School . . . Wiesbaden AB, Germany . . . 1967." Captain Presnall's parting words were: "Keep your head down over there. I sure as hell don't want to see your name on the Vietnam KIA list."

The farewell from the cadre and Air Force guys at the Nimbus was heartwarming. As for Rick Carmen, we'd developed a close working and personal friendship, and I'd especially miss him, along with the other guys.

3RD BATTALION, 187TH INFANTRY, OCTOBER THROUGH NOVEMBER 1967

Following a brief check-in at the 21st Repo Depot for final out-processing, our homeward-bound group was transported to the Rhein-Main Air Base Hotel. We boarded yet another chartered TWA Boeing 720 early the next morning, bound again for McGuire Air Force Base.

United Airlines had a DC-8 departing Philadelphia for San Francisco almost immediately following my arrival at the airport. The flight was a non-revenue repositioning deadhead, so I lucked into a free first-class seat with royalty treatment from the beautiful hostesses.

Dad and Mom awaited me at the gate, and although obviously overjoyed to see their son after ten months, I detected something guarded in their behavior. The first thing that crossed my mind was that something might have happened to

Gary or Boyd. I decided to get to the bottom of whatever was going on and queried Dad for a situation report. "Wizzo, there's a lot of war demonstrators both here in the terminal and outside the main doors. We watched a couple of young Marines just back home from Vietnam having a hard way to go with some hippies awhile ago, and it was all I could do to keep from punching the hippies' lights out. We just don't want you getting into any trouble." That was typical of Dad, worrying about me when the only ones who should have been concerned were the counterculture creeps who might make the fatal mistake of jumping up in his face. Mom was on the verge of bursting into tears and exclaimed, "These people should be ashamed of themselves!"

They were shack on target about the hippies. As I retrieved my aviator's kit and duffle bags from the carousel, a wild-eyed bohemian, probably freaked on LSD and obviously lying in ambush for GIs, provokingly lisped, "Hey *man*, whatcha got in those? Yer assassin's tools?!" That did it. With Mom screaming, "Honey, don't!" I initiated a dash for the scumbag when Dad snatched me by the arms. "Wiz, he's just baiting you for a confrontation. He's probably praying that you'll jump on him so that he can become a martyr with his cronies. Believe me, Wiz, I'd like nothing more than to jerk his pucker string loose and mop the floor with his filthy long hair myself." I momentarily caught the concerned gaze of an airport policeman, who was shaking his head as if to say, "Son, don't do it. I sure don't want to wind up having to haul you off."

Manteca might have been my home of record, but it sure as hell didn't feel like it by then. Greatly contributing to this sensation of nonbelonging was the fact that I no longer really knew anybody. The kids now frequenting the old fast-food hangouts were usually at least one to two years younger, and the few familiar faces weren't exactly trampling over one another to reach my table either. Was it just my imagination, or was I detecting a measure of fear in their expressions?

Gary had wangled a weekend pass shortly prior to my departure, and Dad sat us down for a heart-to-heart talk one afternoon. It was obvious that he was very much afraid of losing either one or both of his sons in Vietnam. He requested a promise that I not volunteer for, as he put it, "duty beyond the norm." Considering his army and OSS participation in World War II, Dad had a very well-rounded knowledge of the combat environment. He was also an early-era poster boy for combat-related post-traumatic stress disorder.

Before I knew it, my time at home once again became a rapidly dwindling commodity. Because of the late hour for check-in at the airport, I was mercifully spared the B-grade counterculture display I'd endured from the freaks two weeks earlier. During the boarding-gate vigil, Dad reached into his coat pocket and removed a small medallion. It was his World War II "ruptured duck" victory pin, and he presented it to me as a token of good luck in combat. Just about then, Mom reactivated the tear ducts, with Dad quickly following suit, and I was speechless. At least Gary was relatively close by at Fort Ord to see Dad and Mom through this very rough initial period of my absence.

The arrival at Nashville Airport several hours later provided a less-than-warm welcome to the state of Tennessee. Proceeding from baggage claim to the army liaison NCO counter in the main terminal for a lift to Fort Campbell, Kentucky, I noticed two unkempt males accompanied by an equally disheveled female watching me from a news stand. I soon found myself ducking and dodging spitballs. The cowards immediately booked for the main terminal, and my first instinct was to chase them down; then I remembered my bags sitting on the floor in open invitation for a rip-off job.

The sixty-mile trip to Fort Campbell was cold and depressing. Among the fourteen or so onboard, most were fresh Fort Benning jump-school graduates whose fear of the unknown was obvious. In my case, the sole fear I harbored was the war reaching its conclusion and leaving me stuck again in a stateside airborne chickenshit garrison.

The 101st Airborne repo depot's first sergeant bellowed, "All personnel in grade E-3 and below fall out to my left!" I instantly deduced that the army caste system was once again manifesting itself, and I sighed with relief in the realization that I was going to be on the right side of the tracks for a change. My rank of SP4 was going to keep me out of the mess-hall grease trap or from engaging in mortal combat with a buffer. I was immediately assigned to Company E (Recon Platoon), 3rd Battalion, 187th Airborne Infantry (The Rakkasans) as a recon squad leader. Now all I had to do was learn what a recon squad leader did.

Echo Company's first sergeant, 1st Sgt. Mac Donald, seemed to be a square-shooting guy, and just as I'd suspected, he confirmed that as with virtually every other unit on post, the company was desperate for junior NCOs. Therefore, he asked if I would be willing to accept an immediate unit promotion to acting sergeant ("acting Jack") as reinforcement to my assignment as a recon squad leader? Like a dummy and desiring to put my best foot forward, I accepted.

Staff Sergeant Rogers was the recon platoon sergeant, and we immediately hit it off surprisingly well. He'd just returned from a tour in Vietnam with the division's 1st Brigade and would remain with the unit to oversee platoon training until our departure. I made it a point to be candid with him, admitting that although I'd usually gravitated toward leadership positions with my peers as a kid, my military leadership experience was virtually nil. He handed me a small infantry-blue army pamphlet titled *The Infantry Squad Leader's Handbook* and suggested I memorize its entire contents.

My roommate and 101st Airborne vet of Vietnam, Hank Richards, had grown up in a northern Montana family of hunting and trapping enthusiasts, and the fieldcraft and tracking skills he taught me well enhanced those imparted by Chris at Fort Bragg. Also in our platoon were two members I'd served with in the Five-O-Nasty, Sgt. Steve Crowder and SP4 Terry Cross. As always, it was comforting to have familiar faces around.

Rumors had been circulating over the division's forming of a long-range patrol (LRP) company, and I'd observed an ominous looking sergeant first class roaming the 2nd Brigade area, attired in jungle fatigues with a Division "Recondo" (reconnaissance/commando) arrowhead brand on his right breast pocket, along with a black ballcap. I'd first seen a similar patch at Bragg called "Raider," and for all I'd known then, it represented archery qualification. The word was that the sergeant first class was a headhunter for the new unit, and I really liked the idea of wearing a black ballcap again. Wishful thinking, I thought: they probably accepted only former Eagle Scouts.

Staff Sergeant Rogers informed me a couple of mornings later that my presence at 2nd Brigade headquarters had been requested by a Sergeant First Class Beck. My name had been selected along with several other company members to be interviewed for possible training and assignment to the division LRP company. From the little I'd heard, LRPs were bloodthirsty fugitives-from-justice psychos with a death wish, sneaking around the jungle in four- to six-man teams and praying for kills. I instantly realized I had to go for it.

Other than a cold, blank stare accompanied by a firm handshake, Sgt. 1st Class Robert Beck wasted no time with socializing. Gesturing toward an adjacent table upon which lay a 1:50,000-scale map, he directed me to identify an object based on an eight-digit grid coordinate he provided. This little problem was a no-brainer, and I quickly determined the correct point, which turned out to be the building I was standing in. I was dead sure that I'd really impressed him with my lack of need to employ the little plastic map protractor, too.

Offering me a seat, Sergeant First Class Beck commenced the interview by stating that LRP duty was strictly voluntary and that were I to survive this session and volunteer, I would be in for extremely physically and mentally demanding training and would probably wash out the first day. He began sizing me up through queries of various military and related subjects, such as whether I had any skeletons locked up in a closet that could prevent my obtaining a secret security clearance and whether I believed that I could kill at very close quarters without hesitation or remorse. Sergeant First Class Beck's facial expression reflected what I believed to be his skepticism over my obviously half-hearted affirmative replies.

"Walker, pretend for a minute that you're a team leader on a LRP mission, far from friendly support, and a young girl pops up out of nowhere asking you for candy. What would your proper course of action be?"

"Well, sergeant, I'd probably give her some candy and instruct her not to mention having seen us."

With an infuriated snarl, he bent over, planted his nose nearly against mine, and yelled, "*Wrong* answer, young sergeant! You'd slit her throat to prevent compromising your team! Don't ever forget this, Walker; anybody over there from eight to eighty can send you, and your entire team, into the afterlife!"

To my utter amazement, Sergeant First Class Beck again shook my hand in parting, stating that I'd been accepted for LRP training at the division recondo school and directed me to return to my unit and start packing—should I so desire. Naturally, I said, "Yes, sergeant!" Unbeknownst to me at the time, my whole life was forever changed that morning on the second floor of 2nd Brigade headquarters.

CHAPTER 4

LRP Training

The Division Recondo School, instituted in the late 1950s by then Maj. Gen. William C. Westmoreland, was situated in the "back 40" of Fort Campbell near an intimidating area known as the Rock Quarry. With our class of sixty-three candidates nervously seated in the bleachers, the commandant of the school, Capt. Peter J. Fitts, paraphrasing the classic movie line, told us, "Okay, assholes, take a look at the man seated on your right and left. Two-and-a-half of you won't be here by this course's end. On behalf of Col. 'Chargin' Charlie' Beckwith, welcome to *my* 101st Airborne Division Recondo School!" Captain Fitts had been a Special Forces NCO in Vietnam, receiving a battlefield commission. With numerous snake and other tattoos from exotic locales writhing down his arms, he would have been equally at home in Oakland's Hell's Angels clubhouse or a longshoremen's bar. Without a doubt, Captain Fitts looked and spoke more like a convict than an "officer and gentleman"—and our youthful student body loved every second of it.

The commandant got down to business by providing a brief rundown as to just why we were there and what we'd be doing over the next three weeks. The first week, Phase I, included preparatory training and evaluation. The two-week-long Phase II consisted of jungle training at the Florida Ranger Camp. Only twelve of us would not fail, we were told.

Captain Fitts turned our motley crew of would-be LRPs over to Staff Sgt. Harold Kaiama, who through appearance and demeanor reminded me very much of Sergeant Burton from basic combat training and First Sergeant Hoolapa from the 509th. "You men are here as volunteers, and the nature of this course and our work demands that you accomplish every task correctly the first time. This job isn't for everybody, and those of you who we identify as being unsuitable will wind up as only a distant memory here. From this moment on, you will address any individual wearing a black ballcap as Ranger, while you in turn will be addressed as Recondo. Additionally, when any cadre member asks the question "What are you?" you will respond with a loud and enthusiastic 'Recondo!'"

The first quality-control eliminator on the agenda was a grueling seven-mile endurance run over uneven terrain. I made it without even needing a third wind and mentally thanked Staff Sergeant Rogers for cutting us no slack on physical training in the 187th. About eight others, mostly from support units, hadn't made the cut and were booted back to their parent units before our noon chow of ice-cold C rations.

Following our gourmet meal was a dead run to the Rock Quarry for a LRP-style swimming lesson. The concept was straightforward enough: negotiate a blindfolded walk twelve feet across a one-foot-wide, twelve-foot-high plank without falling off and breaking your neck, then jump into the ice-cold quarry pond fully clothed and carrying a weapon, and finally swim 150 feet unaided to a dock with the weapon held above water. By my recollection, ten more unfortunates received their walking papers following this confidence test.

Last on our first day's agenda was another fear enticer known as the water-confidence test. No problem to it, just climb a fifty-foot telephone pole to a horizontal eight-by-eight-inch beam, traverse the beam about twenty feet to another telephone pole with a quarter-inch-diameter steel cable extending from it about 200 feet across the pond, monkey-crawl across the cable to its midpoint, then drop into the drink while screaming "Recondo!" A number of candidates refused to even attempt this requirement.

The living accommodations at the Recondo compound were spartan at best, consisting of several Quonset tents. An oil-fired Yukon stove served as our only creature comfort during the subfreezing nights, aiding little in the hang-drying of our soaking wet fatigue uniforms. These stoves were also notorious for starting fires for no apparent reason, so in addition to enduring the discomfort, fire guard duty became another volunteer bonus.

As the training advanced, it became apparent that the entire cadre was top-notch. An NCO who truly stood out among these fine men was Staff Sgt. Roger B. "Hog" Brown, who had already served a tour in Vietnam with the 503rd Infantry and provisional long-range reconnaissance patrol (LRRP) platoon of the 173rd Airborne Brigade and would be accompanying the LRP company back overseas as a team leader and platoon sergeant. In tow with Roger was Sgt. Chris "Turtle" Christenson, who had served with him in Vietnam. Both of these fine soldiers would ultimately become two of my best friends.

A thorough working knowledge of mountaineering was necessary for the job we were to perform in Vietnam, and so we began intensive instruction in the arts of rappelling and rock climbing. We learned the proper procedure for tying a Swiss seat utilizing a twelve-foot, 3,500-pound test sling rope with a snap link ("carabiner") and put this to practical application on the school's fifty-foot rappelling tower and Rock Quarry cliffs. All of this good training with ropes naturally required an intimate knowledge of proper knot usage, and Rangers Brown and Kaiama saw to it that we mastered them all. As with the earlier water drills, we again experienced a number of outright refusals.

Long-range patrol teams routinely found themselves in compromising situations with superior enemy forces, thus necessitating rapid extraction methods. The STABO rig was basically an air force emergency parachute harness modified to accommodate combat gear. The end-riser snap links could readily be attached with one hand to a ladder rung or snap link extended on a line from a helicopter, leaving the other hand free for a weapon. The McGuire rig was a simple extraction device fabricated from a twelve-foot sling rope tied around the chest with a bowline knot and an attached snap link—just hook into the line (commonly called a "string" extraction). Lastly, a contraption known as a "jungle penetrator," a heavy metal affair with shoulder straps and folding arms for a seat, served to bail a team out of really dense stuff.

As with any military training course, individuals tend to strike friendships based on common goals and similar abilities. Thus was born the elite group of SP4 Jim Venable, SP4 Glenn Martinez, PFC Jerry "Cash" Register, PFC James "Willy" Wilson, PFC John Renear, SP4 John "Spaghetti Bender" Gentile, and SP4 Dave Walker. Coincidentally enough, Glenn and I had recently first met while on permanent-change-of-station leave from Germany at the locally famous Freitas Records Store in Stockton, California. We collectively dubbed ourselves "The Magnificent Seven."

Even LRPs had to eat, and the army in its creativity came up with the food packet, long-range patrol (LRP ration). In the interest of conserving weight, these freeze-dried meals came packaged in a waterproof outer bag and could be eaten either rehydrated or in dry form. Included were sundries such as an orange or lemon protein ("John Wayne") bar, cocoa powder, coffee, and other items. My favorite "entrees" were the beef stew and spaghetti with meat sauce.

Because of compulsory noise discipline and the vital ability to detect enemy movement, LRP teams moved at an extremely slow pace—unless being chased—and in extremely dense terrain, a day's movement might cover merely a couple of hundred meters or even less. During low light or night conditions, the point man would be primarily occupied with the detection of booby traps, sometimes necessitating low-crawling and light probing of the trail ahead with fingertips.

Many LRP team encounters with the enemy were of a chance nature. We practiced what seemed to be an endless series of immediate-action front, side, and rear breakaway drills and hasty counterambushes. Newly acquired in our vocabulary was the dark-humored LRP slang term for an ambush: "birthday party."

The first generation of experimental light-intensifying night-vision devices was just entering the army's inventory, and we were familiarized with the still "hush-hush" AN/PVS-2 and 4 Starlight scopes. Unlike infrared equipment—which relies on radiant heat emissions—the Starlight scope magnified existing natural light from the stars and moon, producing a ghostly green image for the viewer. Both versions came equipped with quick-mounting adapters for the M-14/XM-21 and M-16 rifles and worked reasonably well until the operator inadvertently directed the intensifier lens toward a bright light source (such as enemy muzzle flashes) or dropped the thing, causing the unit's automatic shutdown.

Combat/strategic intelligence gathering often required photography, hence our training with the 35-millimeter Honeywell KS-15 reconnaissance camera, which in practice was an absolute user's nightmare because of its complexity. We'd probably be better off with a Minolta, Yashica, or even just an Instamatic, I thought. Turtle Christenson captivated our wide-eyed audience with his hilarious tale of connecting a Claymore detonating wire to an Instamatic camera's flash-firing circuit during a night ambush. Just as the enemy point man reached the Claymore's position, Turtle yelled "Surprise!" as he depressed the shutter button.

Taking into account that LRP teams operated in the enemy's backyard—far from friendly support—we learned the use of several survival items. The ACR-4-F "Firefly" pilot's distress light, a small NiCad battery-powered device, roughly equal in size to a cigarette packet, radiated high-intensity stroboscopic flashes that were clearly visible even during daylight or through a medium fog layer. Another handheld item, the URC-10 UHF pilot's survival radio, featured voice-transmission and aural distress sweep options, similar to the modern-day emergency locator transmitter installed aboard aircraft and seagoing vessels. Included as last resorts were an air force pilot's pyrotechnic distress (pen gun) flare launcher with seven screw-in red star-cluster flares, pilot's distress signaling mirror, and a rubber-coated canvas distress (international orange) VS-17 marker panel. A pilot's survival knife with honing stone and first-aid kit completed our load-bearing equipment complement.

All of this gear had to be carried somehow, and a LRP packed his in a jungle rucksack. Ranger Brown ensured that we learned the proper method for not only packing the 100 pounds of gear we'd be burdened with, but also keeping the various straps and buckles silenced with matte-surface electrical tape. Effective use of available cover and concealment and application of camouflage stick also became second nature.

Because of the classified and extremely disadvantageous (for us!) nature of LRP operations, secure communications were vital. The AN/PRC 25 FM radio was the standard for mission communications, and secure encoding was accomplished through the use of a U.S. KAC encoder/decoder ("KAC wheel") and cipher key list sheets, published by the National Security Agency and changed daily. A plastic device similar in appearance and function to a circular slide rule, the KAC wheel held a given day's encryption sheet, and rotation of the bezel aligned corresponding authentication numbers and letters, which in turn were broadcast by voice or code. The codes were also known as "shacks," and the actual process of encoding outgoing data was commonly referred to as "shacking" or "KAC-ing." Combined with a list of radio frequencies, these items constituted our signal operating instructions.

It was an unavoidable fact of life that LRP teams were occasionally liquidated and sometimes outright disappeared. Ranger Brown solemnly stated the starkly simple radio procedure for a team facing imminent destruction: just transmit the team's call sign with "Timber . . . timber . . . timber!" and the word would quickly get around in the rear that the team's next extraction would more than likely be a body-recovery mission, assuming there were any bodies to recover.

SP5 Jim Fleck, himself a recent LRRP veteran of Vietnam as well as a combat medic, provided us with top-notch instruction in field first aid, placing heavy emphasis on the initial life-saving steps (clear the airway, stop the bleeding, check for wounds, treat for shock). We also learned to administer morphine and atropine and to properly employ an albumen (blood expander) IV when necessary. Though it was rarely encountered, Jim brought up the issue of snakebites during a mission. Our survival kits contained snakebite treatments, but no antivenin, and as Jim put it, a cobra, krait, or bamboo viper (nicknamed "two-step") would have the victim meeting his creator in forty to sixty minutes. Of minor reassurance was Jim's comment that most snakes preferred a hasty retreat unless cornered.

Absolute confidence and total proficiency in the proper handling and employment of military explosives were required. The instructor, Staff Sgt. George Brubaker (also known as "Cool Bru" or "Doc"), was a friendly, although spooky, individual who had served with Special Forces in the Phoenix and Delta Projects. We mastered the methods for constructing mechanical and electrical ambushes with C-4, TNT, Claymores, grenades, and other explosives. Ranger Brubaker's demonstration of the M-14 TH3 thermite grenade really got our attention. With a peak burn temperature of about 4,000 degrees Fahrenheit, it melted its way from the top to bottom of a jeep engine block in seconds. He cautioned us that the flame's brilliance could cause retinal damage.

Rangers Brubaker and Brown also taught us the finer points of silent enemy elimination with the Gerber Mark II fighting knife and the garrote. An excellent garrote could be fabricated from a two-foot length of 550-pound-test parachute suspension line or C ration case wire, with hardwood dowels for grips. Just creep up on your target's back, run the line over his head in a cross-over on the neck, plant a knee in the small of his back, and pull with all you had. Unarmed techniques were also emphasized, and we had the controversial and lethal choke hold—the sleeper hold—down to a science long before the LAPD did.

Long-range patrol teams had a requirement for an amphibious-infiltration capability, and the Rock Quarry served as the area for our RB-15 rubber reconnaissance boat training. As it turned out, the boats were an entertaining respite from the laborious syllabus, and we frolicked in the freezing water during seemingly endless capsize drills.

Map reading and land navigation were treated as a religion by the cadre, and we became intimately familiar with military maps on a global scale. Now we'd be dealing with computation of position through breakdown of polar coordinates originating from lines of latitude and longitude. I'd learned the use of a pace cord in advanced individual training, but as the cadre put it, pace cords were, for all intents and purposes, useless in mountainous triple-canopy jungle terrain. Rather, the key to avoiding getting lost lay in constant map-terrain comparison and periodic position fixes through compass intersection or resection. This often entailed scaling some very high trees, we were told. Bare-bones direction determination by reference to stars and planets was a last resort, and we acquired the basics. Ranger Brown and Turtle drove home the reality that every student would have an opportunity to display land-navigation proficiency in Florida—and happy trails to the unfortunate soldier who plotted a bum course.

With our having received a firm grounding in the basics, extensive classroom instruction was allotted for the meticulous preplanning and coordination of a LRP operation. When all was said and done, we were composing and reciting operations and patrol orders in our sleep.

The Fort Campbell phase reached its conclusion, and along with about twenty-nine other LRP hopefuls, I was elated to still be in the running. Now all I had to do was survive the two weeks in Florida.

We boarded a C-130 at Campbell Army Airfield for the flight to Eglin Air Force Base and the nearby Florida Ranger Camp, otherwise known as Camp Rudder. Located east-north-east of Pensacola on the Gulf Coast of Florida, Camp Rudder boasted what we'd all come to lovingly know as the Black Bay Swamp Region. During the flight, Ranger Kaiama cheerfully suggested that we just think of the training as a guest appearance on Mutual of Omaha's *Wild Kingdom*.

Camp Rudder featured a small combination snack bar/PX called the Gator Lounge. Most of us purchased Gerber MK II combat knives, which we promptly strapped to our calves to obtain the maximum macho effect. The cadre delayed informing us that wearing the thing in such a manner guaranteed its immediate loss in dense jungle.

The PT continued without mercy, and Ranger Kaiama presented us with a new challenge, the twenty-five-foot rope climb. During his demonstration, he ascended the unknotted rope solely through the employment of upper body strength and hands only, giving a stuffed gorilla secured to a tree branch a love pat on the belly. I'd been a fair rope climber in high-school gym class—that is, using the old interlocked-feet method. I was able to make it hand-over-hand slightly shy of halfway up before running out of steam. At least virtually everyone else encountered this shortcoming. The trick, as we discovered, was to keep the elbows close into the body and take small footlong bights on the rope. After numerous off-duty practice sessions, most of us made it to the top, if only barely.

The Black Bay Swamp, featuring a mock "aggressor" enemy force, awaited us eager candidates, and Ranger Randolph supervised our first overnight patrol, manned by Jerry Register, John Pratt, Jim Venable, Willie Wilson, and yours truly. Just prior to sunset, our motley crew was infiltrated via three-quarter-ton truck into a godforsaken area of marshes, brambles, and cattails, well sheltered by dense overhanging weeping willow and cypress trees. As luck would have it, Ranger Randolph pointed his finger at me, stating: "Recondo Walker, you are my first victim. You're the team leader now, and this is our present position . . . take us to this grid coordinate for our night defensive position." Our destination was about 1.5 kilometers through all of this stuff, and here I was already tiptoeing around trying to avoid imaginary alligators and snakes—a real leader of men. Two sensory items that immediately caught my attention were the stench of decaying vegetation and probably alligator shit.

The cadre's intent with these shock-leadership appointments was to determine if we could think on our feet, and I made a valiant attempt to appear as if I knew what I was doing. Prior to departing the insertion point, I assigned order-of-march positions and reviewed the immediate action drill for enemy contact. Considering the relatively flat terrain, I prudently elected to employ a pace cord. Plotting what I hoped to be an accurate course, we stumbled off into the wet and dark jungle void.

I quickly determined that placing Pratt on the point position was a mistake, despite his ongoing claims to being a hot-shot Louisiana swamp-beast tamer. Aside from moving like a bull through a china shop, he whimpered like a beaten child. Pratt's biggest shortcomings, however, lay in his unabated second-guessing of my navigation and his constant noise-discipline violations. Ranger Randolph, having seen and heard enough, replaced Pratt with Wilson on point.

Our team conducted three more overnight missions in the Black Bay Swamp, during which we managed not to get caught by the aggressors. Quite to the contrary, we ambushed a squad, and I called a passable simulated artillery fire mission on a platoon-size element.

It seemed that almost as soon as the Florida phase had started, we were on a C-130 back to Fort Campbell. The onboard atmosphere resembled a funeral parlor, with everyone wondering who had or hadn't been selected. The instructors sure hadn't given anything up.

Captain Fitts held a final formation at the Recondo School compound that afternoon, thanking every man for putting out his best. He told us, "I'd be proud to bust bush with any man in this formation." For the twelve of us who made the final cut, we had merely earned a learner's permit for LRP operations. The finishing school would soon convene in Vietnam.

Now came the moment of truth with the school's sergeant major reading the unit acceptance roster. Frankly, I was in a cloud during the reading. Renear, Venable, Wilson, Brown (Lacy), Penchanksky, Register, Ortegon, McChesney, Martinez, and two more barely registered until I disbelievingly heard my name. Graduation from airborne school had been the proudest moment in my life up to this point, but this boosted me off the scales. I'd just been officially recognized and accepted into a very small fraternity of special men.

Out of respect for those who hadn't been selected, the cadres delayed awarding the simple perks for which we new LRPs had toiled, sweat, and bled until they departed. Upon being issued our genuine new Rawlings black ballcaps and a spare Recondo brand, we virgin LRPs were directed to return to our parent units, pack, and report to the LRP company barracks in the Division HHC building.

A few of us jumped in a taxi back to main post, instructing the driver to head for the tailor shop. We sure wouldn't want to get caught without the Recondo brand loudly and proudly sewn on our right breast pockets. The price for attaining this high honor, which I considered an absolute bargain, was the swapping of my acting sergeant's stripes for the old SP4.

CHAPTER 5

Vietnam

Captain Fitts rounded us all up the next morning for a SITREP. We'd be departing Campbell Army Airfield on a C-141 aircraft for Vietnam on December 3, and our routing would take us via Travis Air Force Base in California, Wake Island, and Clark Air Base in the Philippines to Bien Hoa Air Base in Vietnam. We'd have only fifteen working days to get equipment, finish last-minute packing, and raise final hell on post.

Top Walker and the senior NCOs had assembled tentative team assignments, and I drew Team 2-1, with Sgt. Roy Caughorn as team leader. Roy was a very imposing and colorful individual who had received a serious AK-47 bullet wound through the mouth during an earlier LRRP tour in Vietnam. Jim Fleck, the class's first-aid instructor, would be returning to Vietnam with us in the dual roles of company medic and assistant team leader. The low-ranker cherries consisted of PFC Jim Wilson, SP4 Richard Sachs, and SP4 Dave Walker. Out of sheer luck, we inherited Staff Sgt. Roger B. "Hog" Brown as our 2nd Platoon sergeant.

The day before departure arrived. Everyone had finished packing, completing last wills and testaments, SGLI beneficiaries, and so on, and we LRPs decided to throw a party at the 2nd Brigade enlisted men's club. By territorial rights, we were the guests, since the majority of club patrons hailed from the 187th, 501st, and 506th Infantry units. Well, the LRP mentality dictated that we were *nobody's* guests, especially on our last night in the states, and through unanimous agreement we proceeded to place the club under new management.

"D" Day dawned, and Top Walker gathered us together for a brief informational session in the afternoon. As per Captain Fitts's orders, all company members were to write their families a letter stating safe arrival in Vietnam at the soonest opportunity. Really newsworthy was that a detachment from the Royal Australian Special Air Service would be residing with us and training us at Camp Ray (Bien Hoa); they would also accompany us to Bear Cat during our acclimatization period for additional training with the 9th Infantry Division LRP Company. The division's 1st Brigade had of course been in-country since mid-1965, and we'd be absorbing a number of original 1/101st LRRP members. To a man, we newbies realized that between the SAS and 1/101st LRRP guys, we'd have a library of combat survival experience to reference.

A moderately dense radiation fog layer blanketed Campbell Airfield's pitch-dark ramp, creating a surreal effect emanating from the alternating white-white-green swaths of the airport's rotating identification beacon. I instinctively realized that we were participating in an historical event and had stocked up on plenty of film and flash cubes for the Instamatic.

Loud cheers erupted as our Starlifter broke ground, and I believe we were all simultaneously struck by the fact that this was for real: the next dawn we'd witness would be somewhere northeast of Wake Island. Our great adventure had begun.

The touchdown at Travis after a four-hour flight was a welcome respite, and we were allowed to disembark and grab quick snacks in the MAC aerial port squadron terminal cafeteria. I nearly experienced cardiac arrest upon noting the burritos and corn dogs on the menu, and I jumped at the opportunity to stock up for long the flight.

Other than a couple of piss calls, I slept like a comatose skid-row bum for the entire trip from Travis to Wake. We were rudely awakened by the loadmaster's PA announcement to check seatbelts, and with the aircraft descending ever lower towards the ocean surface, I wondered just where in the hell the airport was. When it appeared as if the engine nacelle intakes were just about to ingest seawater, a rush of whitecaps breaking against coral reefs whizzed blurrily by the window, and we were on the ground a split second later.

Disembarking the aircraft, we were greeted with a beautiful South Pacific day of about eighty degrees and a light salty sea breeze. The sparseness of the airport was a minor shock. Our lone C-141 sat on the ramp having its affairs tended to, and a simple two-story beige terminal building with wooden silver block letters reading WAKE ISLAND AIRFIELD stood isolated at the ramp's northeast edge. Actually, this understated structure held great historical significance as it had originally been erected by Pan American World Airways as a hotel in the mid-1930s to facilitate their Boeing China Clipper operations.

Once again airborne for Clark Air Base, I was captivated by the boundless expanse of the Pacific Ocean. Every so often, I was able to glimpse an opposite-direction aircraft with gracefully streaming contrails or a toy ship seven miles below. Around six hours out of Wake, I began sighting small atolls, and we eventually emerged into a major landfall in the distance. I correctly guessed this to be Luzon, home of Manila and Clark Air Base.

A crew bus transported our weary bodies to the MAC terminal for some much-needed leg stretching and hot food. Totally unlike Wake, this place had wall-to-wall civilian and military transports as well as fighter aircraft. Clearly visible about fifty miles to the north was Mount Pinatubo, an active volcano. I sure hoped that Pinatubo wouldn't pull another Krakatoa or Vesuvius until we were once again airborne and well out of the area.

The silence was deafening during the final leg to Vietnam. About twenty minutes before touchdown at Bien Hoa, the landmass became clearer. Willy provided an exciting commentary on the columns of dark black smoke rising from the inland mountainous areas, the origin of which, according to Sergeant Caughorn, were air or artillery strikes, possibly even B-52 strikes. This revelation naturally attracted rubber-neckers. The war had finally become a reality for us.

The cabin erupted in cheers, catcalls, and finger whistles as the main landing gear trucks contacted the runway. Like everyone onboard, I was excited about our arrival on Vietnamese soil—and more than casually curious about what awaited us outside the cabin doors.

Our premonitions of doom and gloom were all for naught. The outside air temperature was hanging around ninety degrees, with high humidity, but it wasn't unbearable. Most importantly, nobody was shooting at us (yet!). Army buses met us at the aircraft, and the first item that sparked my curiosity was the cyclone fence wire welded to the window ports. Sergeant Caughorn said it was so that no one could throw in a frag or satchel charge.

None of us were prepared for the third-world squalor we encountered during the short ride to Camp Ray. The people traveled unpaved streets littered with trash and animal waste and lived in shanties constructed from corrugated sheet metal, flattened beverage cans, and cardboard C-ration cases. The stench from open-air sewers and rotting fish was overpowering, worsened by exhaust from two-stroke Lambretta "cyclo buses" and cow-dung cooking fires. Also prominent was a scent none of us fresh arrivals had smelled: burning human excrement and diesel oil. Amidst all of this chaos and confusion was the unmistakable *whup-whup* of Huey helicopter blades.

Totally contradictory to these conditions were the beautiful young women dressed in alluring white silk *ao-dai* slit skirts, as were the Honda "female 50" motorcycles being ridden by all age groups. In his heavily Hispanic accent, Ortegon seized the moment to quote the early-1960s TV commercial line "You meet the nicest people on a Honda." Sergeant Caughorn reflexively countered, "Yeah? Well, one or more of those nice people is most likely at this very moment plotting a way to blow our asses into kingdom-come along with this bus."

I had noticed several of what appeared to be small army-navy shops along our route and voiced my curiosity about why I was seeing U.S.-manufactured combat equipment for sale by the

Vietnamese. Ranger Brubaker answered the question in no uncertain terms: "Okay, here's another object lesson for all of you cherries. When you lose a piece of gear, this is where it usually winds up, and more than likely an enemy gook will sooner or later turn it right back on you out in the bush. As for these shop owners, most of them are enemy personnel to begin with."

As we entered the Camp Ray compound, I heard a loud thunder overhead. Looking straight up, I was treated to the spectacle of an F-100 Super Sabre fighter executing victory rolls in afterburner over the Bien Hoa runway. All of us had been attracted to the show, and I wondered where he'd just been. Maybe he'd even knocked down a MiG or two.

If we'd imagined Camp Ray as a collection of snake- and rat-infested thatched huts in the middle of the jungle rain forest, the reality of semipermanent facilities was a pleasant surprise and immense relief. The ground-level, single-story buildings known as "hooches," were of frame-and-slat construction, with corrugated metal roofs, bordered and topped with sandbags. Optimistically, the sandbags were present to partially absorb small-arms, mortar, and rocket impacts.

The remainder of the first day was devoted to moving into our fourteen-man living quarters and getting the lay of the land while absorbing the fact that we were really here. These airy structures comfortably housed two six-man teams in the main living area, with a separate plywood cubicle for the primary and assistant team leaders. Team 2-2 would be sharing our new home, and it was good to have Turtle, who had been assigned as 2-2's assistant team leader, as a hoochmate. I had noted blocks of rat poison placed around the immediate hooch perimeters and casually commented to Jim Fleck that I could do without rats to begin with. Jim remarked that the rats weren't the big problem; the snakes that they attracted were— which really had me tip-toeing for a while.

Even LRPs had to surrender to nature every so often, and we had a four-hole outhouse in the hooch area. Beneath each hole was the lower half of a fifty-gallon drum, which could be readily removed from a rear hatch. The waste within the container was then generously doused with diesel fuel or gasoline and ignited, creating the much-revered fatigue duty known as "shit-burning detail." Although likely only "shithouse" legend, it had been long circulated that a number of persons had blown themselves sky high through tossing lit cigarettes into the drums, which still contained residual fuel, during their constitutionals.

Staff Sgt. "Hutch" Hutchinson, our unit supply NCO, made a valiant effort to accommodate our creature comforts through a double issue of poncho liners (jungle camouflage tropical nylon blankets), stateside-issue pillows and cases, and a mosquito net to each man—a configuration that turned out to be surprisingly comfortable on our wood-and-canvas cots.

The 17th Cavalry Regiment's mess hall was responsible for feeding us, and our first meal in Southeast Asia consisted of surprisingly good roast beef with mashed potatoes and gravy. Ranger Brown, with his wry sense of humor, attempted to spoil the meal by stating that what we believed to be roast beef was most likely water buffalo or dog meat. Some of the guys complained about the reconstituted milk, which I actually thought was almost good.

A small number of the combat-tested 1/101st LRRP veterans looked down at us with disdain. A couple of the old guys would say things like, "I've already paid my dues in this place and I'm not in the business of breaking in cherries." Sadly, these discontented original LRRP veterans, whom we newbies intensely respected, opted for DEROS back to the U.S. or transferred to line units.

Team 2-1's first night in our new Southeast Asian home wasn't without its surprises. I'd just dozed off into a peaceful slumber when an ear-splitting *bam* reverberated through the compound. Sachs yelled that we were being attacked as we all dove for whatever negligible cover might be available under our cots. Turtle commenced laughing uncontrollably, exclaiming, "Take it easy, you paranoid cherry clowns. It's just a 105 howitzer battery over by the air base firing some H&I [harassment and interdiction] rounds at suspected gook positions!" Thanks for warning us! Personally, I hoped this wasn't to be our typical first-call method.

Sergeant Hutch came through for us with an issue of Vietnamese tiger-stripe combat uniforms. Frankly, they looked good for profiling purposes and definitely made one look like a walking bush, but the closely woven and thick all-cotton material had the wearer in a dehydrating sweat after the slightest exertion. Light-weight cotton-polyester blend rip-stop jungle-leaf-pattern uniforms of American manufacture existed, but as Hutch angrily informed us, the Air Force police of all people had rerouted—i.e., stolen—incoming shipments. We were all rapidly picking up on the drift that strange things happened in Vietnam.

The U.S. might have been known as "The Land of the Big PX," but the facility on Camp Ray totally contradicted the phrase. Plainly stated, the place was immense not only in physical dimension, but also content. Within its high-output air-conditioned confines were what seemed like endless rows of Akai, Sony, and Teac reel-to-reel tape recorders, shelves jammed with high-end Minolta, Yashica, and Pentax cameras, and anything else a young GI with money burning a hole in his pocket could desire.

The opportunity finally came to zero our weapons, and the Aussies joined in on the festivities. The standard SAS shoulder weapon was the Australian version of the Belgian FN FAL self-loading rifle, which fired a standard 7.62-millimeter NATO round. Gas-operated and with a magazine capacity of twenty rounds, it was very similar to our own M-14 service rifle. Out of interservice courtesy and curiosity, we swapped turns with one another's weapons on the range, and the Aussies took obvious joy in their good-natured criticism over our "toy" rifles: "Blimey, blokes! This li'l bugger is made plum outta bloomin' plastic!"

Rangers Brubaker and Brown assembled us all later in the afternoon for a short familiarization class on the XM-21 sniper rifle and Hi-Standard .22 LR Supermatic semi-auto target pistol, two weapons we'd only heard about. The XM-21 was basically an accurized match-grade M-14 with a Sionics silencer and Redfield 3x9 "Accurange" scope. The Hi-Standard had a ten-round total capacity, including one round chambered, and was equipped with a silencer. Employing hollow-point rounds, the pistol would put an eternal hurt on an unfortunate enemy target. Unlike the silenced weapons we had seen in Hollywood productions, the real things weren't actually silenced, but rather suppressed. A medium-intensity *pop* and the mechanical action of the weapon were clearly audible. We were informed that each team leader would be equipped with the Hi-Standard and that arrangements were being made with the 9th Infantry Division to send one member of each team to their sniper school in Bear Cat. Naturally, I strove to make both NCOs aware that I was a deadeye shot and would the powers-that-be please consider me for sniper training.

In addition to the M-16, I was assigned an M-79 with the stock sawed-off to a pistol grip, which would be secured to my rucksack during missions. After expending about forty rounds of high explosive at an old three-quarter-ton truck target about 300 meters downrange, I had the technique of range estimation down pretty well and felt fairly confident in my ability to actually hit something with this overgrown shotgun. The weapon was equipped with an adjustable flip-up post-sight, but as Sergeant Caughorn put it, I wouldn't have time to be dilly-dallying with setting a sight during a combat situation.

The SAS boys always stressed in their boasting that deadly snakes were an everyday part of life in the homeland. To prove the point, one of their corporals departed the compound one morning in search of a suitably venomous snake to play with. He returned a couple of hours later, nearly blind-drunk, with the meanest and ugliest seven-foot jet-black forest cobra that had probably ever slithered the planet. Most unnerving was the totally nonchalant manner in which the corporal handled this murderous reptile. As for we cherry Yanks, to a man, all we hoped was that these fanged assassins weren't really all that simple to blunder into, and I can't recall one of us taking up the Aussie offers to teach us the finer points of snake-handling.

Immediately following the Aussie corporal's snake-handling demo, Ranger Brown gathered all cherries for a private reality check. "Guys, I know that you all got a big kick of that guy's show and that he meant well. Bear this in mind, however. This country as well as virtually all of Southeast Asia is chock full of deadly snakes, especially forest and king cobras. An old joke goes something like, How does one piss off a cobra? The answer is that one can't . . . because they're born and stay pissed off to begin with. If you stumble onto one, just back off, and he'll move on. Having said that, should you encounter a female nesting her eggs, run, don't walk, as she'll be in hot pursuit and chasing you out of Dodge." Considering that Jim Fleck had told us virtually the same thing during our Recondo training, we took this other highly experienced combat veteran's advice to heart.

Team 2-1 was assigned a brief training mission outside the southern Camp Ray compound in an area named Buu Long. We infiltrated on foot to a narrow trail departure point outside the wire, leading into thick bramble and rubber trees on moist ground. This was to be our first exposure to actual hostile territory and also our initiation in the carrying of live high-explosive grenades. Sergeant Caughorn reminded us to maintain high vigilance and noise discipline, taking care not to touch anything manmade or unnatural. As we'd already been taught, the gooks loved booby-trapping items such as dud explosive rounds and combat equipment, not to mention dead bodies.

We'd been moving extremely slowly for about an hour, my position in the line of march being point slack for Sergeant Caughorn, when I detected a reddish-brown rifle stock approximately four meters to my right front. Freezing in my tracks and not quite believing what I was seeing, I took another step, making eye contact with an equally startled young enemy soldier with an AK-47 wearing pea-green shorts and foreign-looking web gear. As I reflexively snapped my weapon in the soldier's direction, Sergeant Caughorn frantically waved his palm at me in a halting gesture, just as the gook took off in a dead run. In a low whisper, I asked Sergeant Caughorn what was wrong, and he replied that although the enemy we'd encountered might have been merely a trail watcher, he could also have been an advance scout for a much larger force. Consequently, I could have started something bigger than we could handle, with the distinct possibility of our being caught in a crossfire from the paranoid perimeter guards at Camp Ray. We weren't packing enough ammo and ordnance to develop, much less sustain, an extended firefight.

Sergeant Caughorn instructed Willy, already grabbing the handset, to call in the sighting to our tactical operations center, and Captain Fitts ordered the team back to Camp Ray for a debriefing. Sergeant Caughorn and Jim had obviously sensed something we newbies hadn't, and Sergeant Caughorn whispered to everyone that he thought the soldier was NVA. We heard a series of semi-auto gunshots about 200 meters to our west, and I noted the expressions of distress on Jim's and Sergeant Caughorn's faces. Jim identified the shots as coming from an AK and said the soldier was signaling his buddies. That definitely got our attention. Sergeant Caughorn instructed Sachs, who was assigned as drag, to "Check six like all of our lives depend on it! We're probably gonna get chased for a spell!"

Our fears weren't unfounded. We could clearly hear gooks breaking bush and conversing in normal tones uncomfortably close behind us, and when their blind automatic-weapons fire began, I personally cringed in anticipation of catching an AK-47 slug in the back. So this was what it was like being a target. I instantaneously learned the distinct and unmistakable loud *crack* a bullet makes in flight. Worse yet was the shrill blast of a police whistle, which even I knew indicated a commander maneuvering his force. At least I wasn't alone as the rest of the guys appeared no calmer than me. The gooks seemed to be gaining ground on us, and Sergeant Caughorn loudly whispered: "Immediate action rear, and then we haul ass!"

As he'd been trained, Sachs, pulling rear security, immediately faced rearward and emptied a twenty-round magazine in the enemy's direction, followed by pitching an M-26 frag. Sachs then beelined for Sergeant Caughorn's point position as the remainder of us followed suit with Sachs's initial actions. Without being told, Willy again contacted our tactical operations center as a reminder that we were presently on the run and that the perimeter people not fire us up. Well, I'd asked for excitement and had gotten it, hadn't I?

The gooks weren't backing off, and during our hyper-vigilant running battle back to the Camp Ray perimeter, I realized just how much self-discipline and situational awareness Sergeant Caughorn had exhibited in preventing my firing up the first gook. His buddies would most likely have been on top of us before we'd even realized it.

The situation became more desperate when we heard a series of *bang-whoosh* sounds accompanied by loud detonations and thick black clouds of smoke with buzzing shrapnel and disintegrating vegetation. Sergeant Caughorn yelled that they were probing us with RPG-7 rockets. He snatched the radio handset from Wilson, informing the tactical operations center that we required chopper gunship support *now.*

We continued our escape until hearing the lifesaving rotor beats of two inbound UH-1C gunships from the 101st Aviation Company. "Team 2-1, pop smoke, over." Sergeant Caughorn pitched a yellow smoke grenade as far as he could in our pursuers' direction, and the lead chopper came back with "We have mellow yellow, how copy?" Caughorn informed the birds that we had no positive information about how many or where the gooks were and that they should fire up the place for all it was worth, just not between the smoke and Bien Hoa perimeter unless we instructed otherwise. As soon as the smoke canister had struck the deck, we continued the dead-run for an additional 200 meters to escape the danger-close zone from the chopper guns and rockets, and Sergeant Caughorn ordered that we set up a tight wagon-wheel defensive perimeter until the birds made their first run in. Caughorn gestured with two fingers to his eyes to keep a sharp watch as the gooks might split forces and attempt sweeping or encircling us. With the first volley from the choppers, Caughorn ordered me to pop a red smoke to mark our position, and upon executing another IA drill, we resumed the egress to Camp Ray.

What looked and sounded like a daylight Fourth of July commenced with the choppers firing up the place with their quad M-60 machine guns and 2.75-inch rockets. Clearly audible over the radio were the chopper crews exchanging curses over taking small-arms hits from the gooks. The choppers must have done a real job on the gooks as we didn't hear another peep out of them. With trembling limbs and rapidly beating hearts, we made it back to Camp Ray while the getting was good.

What I personally learned on that first contact mission was that (1) I wouldn't panic and (2) I had been ready to drop the first and only sighted gook in his tracks. I'd acquired a first taste of being the hunter (and hunted), and although frightening, that same wonderful adrenaline rush had coursed through my veins. I'd finally seen the elephant.

Captain Fitts and our intelligence NCO, Staff Sergeant Brubaker, conducted the debriefing, which seemed more like a Gestapo interrogation. Along with the rest of our team, I was prodded with numerous questions. Was I sure of what I'd seen? Did his uniform, gear, and weapon look new or worn? Did he look healthy or more like he'd just been liberated from Buchenwald? What direction did he take during his breaking of contact with you? How many of his buddies would you estimate were tracking you? Team 2-1's egos received priceless boosts at the interview's conclusion with our leaders' congratulations on our accurate observations.

Our contact had generated further fire missions from a perimeter 4.2-inch mortar platoon and the Bien Hoa 105 battery. A line infantry company from the 501st Infantry performed a bomb-damage assessment on the area, yielding about thirty enemy KIA and beaucoup captured weapons and explosives. Sergeant Caughorn told us that his gut feeling was that something big was brewing—which would soon prove to be an understatement.

Team 2-1 naturally became the talk of the compound over the engagement, and we constantly fielded wide-eyed questions about whether it was scary or whether we had shot any gooks. Attempting to maintain an air of nonchalance, we played down the fear factor but disappointingly had to come clean on the second issue. Maybe we'd tagged somebody during the IA drills, maybe not. More than likely, the choppers, 4.2 platoon, and Redleg had taken out the gooks. Sure, Team 2-1 had just been elevated to the top of the company's newbie pyramid, but actually seeing an enemy soldier and exchanging fire were the true tests we all sought.

Winding down in our hooch later on, I chanced to overhear Sergeant Caughorn and Jim Fleck discussing the day's activities and we low-rankers' performance during the mission. When my name came up, Jim matter-of-factly stated that I might be slightly trigger-happy but would most likely be okay with some seasoning. Sachs had impressed both of our leaders with his lightning-quick performance during the first IA maneuver, and Willy had been solid and cool on the radio. The general consensus was that we had a pretty good team in the making. Most importantly in my mind, I'd earned legitimate bragging rights to having been the first cherry in F/58 LRP to engage in a stare-down contest—albeit brief—with a real live enemy soldier, and I was also among the first three to engage in a firefight. Admittedly, I felt somewhat short-changed over not having been allowed to cancel the gook's ticket, which would have instantaneously elevated me to the status of "top cherry." As for the gooks' purpose in having been out there in the first place, it became obvious a few weeks later that they'd been probing defenses and scouting infiltration routes for the 1968 Tet Offensive.

In what became a common evening spectacle, the 105 battery would pump out illumination rounds to light up the outer areas for an AC-47 gunship nicknamed "Puff the Magic Dragon." The gook activity was increasing at an alarming rate outside the wire, and Puff would work an assigned area over with his three 7.62-millimeter Vulcan mini-guns. Reportedly, one mini-gun could cover the entire area of a football field with merely a one-foot gap. Although every fifth round was a tracer, the gun's 6,000-rounds-per-minute rate of fire created the illusion of steady streams of flame. The throaty roar of the guns was deafening.

Being the true wild man that he was, Captain Fitts scheduled a "morale"—i.e., brothel—run for us in Long Binh, located about six miles south of Camp Ray. We'd heard tales (unfounded) about the incurable "black syph," also known as the "galloping goose step," which had incapacitated GIs to the extent of their being sent to some top-secret leper-like colony on Okinawa, forever thereafter being listed as missing in action. Bearing this in mind and considering the extremely unhygienic conditions present in the "house of joy," I decided to pass on a potentially meaningful relationship, opting instead for a simple pud-pulling at the bargain rate of one buck.

During the rough and dusty ride back to Camp Ray, Al Contreros zeroed in on an older "papa-san" to our right front riding a Honda. He wore the stereotypical conical "gook sampan hat," and as we overtook him on a bridge across rice paddy rows, Al thought fast and grabbed our driver's push broom. Just as we came abeam of the papa san, Al placed the broom's bristle end under the rear of the old man's hat and raised it, the force of the oncoming wind locking the hat to his face and totally blocking his vision. We all burst into hysterical laughter over the spectacle that followed: the old man reflexively released the handlebars to raise his hat, and the bike immediately broke right, jumped the bridge's curb, and took wing into the paddies about fifteen feet below. The papa-san trailed closely behind the smoke-belching bike in a double cartwheel splash-down. I don't believe that any of us aboard the truck desired that the old man be injured, and we were relieved to see him stand up, screaming and shaking his fists in defiance at our departing truck. Ranger Brubaker made a command decision that knowledge of the incident remain restricted to those who'd witnessed it. I remember thinking that we sure weren't going to be winning any hearts and minds through pulling stunts like this.

With slightly over two weeks in Vietnam, the company relocated to Bear Cat, home of the 9th Infantry Division and its Long-Range Patrol Company, located to the southwest in the IV Corps Tactical Area. The purpose of our week-long trip was twofold: pick up lessons learned in-country by the 9th Division guys and participate in joint-unit advanced jungle operations training provided by the SAS.

The 9th Division LRPs provided us a warm welcome in their combined enlisted men and NCO club, and over fresh Budweisers, they dazzled us with their tales of combat in the Mekong River Delta. Rather than enduring the hardships of humping triple-canopy Central Highland jungle rain forest, the 9th Infantry guys languished in endless conditions of wetness, filth, and stifling humidity in disease-ridden and mosquito- and snake-infested swamps. With both units being highly competitive in nature, we engaged in beer chug-a-lug contests and wrestling matches, all the while respecting the dividing line between these combat veterans and us.

The SAS had an abundance of nasty tricks in their book and enthusiastically imparted them to our attentive class. Through decades of jungle fighting against the Japanese in the Pacific and rebel factions in Africa, they had learned to think like the enemy, and they deluged us with information, such as how to construct nonexplosive booby traps. The punji stake pit, fabricated from sharpened bamboo stalks and placed angularly in a camouflaged hole, worked well for incapacitating a soldier. The Malaysian foot snare, a suitably strong single or woven vine with one end secured to a bent tree branch for spring action, caught an unwary soldier by an ankle and fatally swung his body into a punji or a spike-studded tree. Similar principles applied with other equally diabolical devices, a number of which employed home-made arrows and spears. Blowguns and crossbows with poison-tipped darts and bolts could also be extremely effective, with the added advantage of total silence. Got an empty ammo can handy? Great, toss in a pissed-off cobra or krait. The possibilities were endless, limited only by one's imagination and skill. And most of the required materials existed in nature.

With the 9th Division guys along for security and moral support, we participated in two one-day practice missions and one overnight practice mission in known enemy areas. Recent indicators of enemy presence, such as fresh sandal tracks and warm cooking fire sites, were discovered, but we encountered no gooks. None of us slept a wink on the night mission, and personally, I imagined killer snakes slithering over me in the darkness. The fun part was that we had been infiltrated with full combat gear and ammo/ordnance loads via Huey helicopters, just like real grownup LRPs. Not so fun was setting up live Claymore mine widowmaker ambushes. We had witnessed the destructive capability of these devices in training, and the instructors had relentlessly emphasized the necessity for doing everything by the numbers. So, assuming we did everything right, there was always the distinct possibility of a smart gook counter-booby-trapping our booby-trap. Just turn the Claymore back on us, or even more diabolically yet, bury a U.S. frag grenade under the Claymore and *kaboom* during retrieval. And as if that wasn't bad enough, all a team needed was a nearby lightning strike to energize the mine's electrical blasting cap.

Just prior to departing Bear Cat, we had been practicing immediate-action drills in an immense bamboo forest. The exercise coincided with our first live exposure to the M-15 white-phosphorous grenade, and we managed to start one hell of a fire. The M-15 suffered from numerous shortcomings, not the least of which was its three-second delayed fuse. It also had a nasty habit of uncommanded activation because of the unstable chemical and flimsy sheet metal casing. And if one were unfortunate enough to come in contact with the high-temperature burning material, its lack of need for oxygen would quickly have the victim screaming for mercy as the chemical unabatedly bored holes through his clothing and body. Captain Fitts made a command decision following this incident, forever banning the use of white-phosphorous grenades.

We returned to Camp Ray on Christmas Eve a little savvier, and the folks had sent me a $50.00 check for Christmas. Out of wishful thinking, I stuffed the check into my wallet to cash back in the World eleven months in the future.

The 17th Cavalry mess hall pulled out all the stops in preparing our first Christmas dinner in Vietnam, and we voraciously feasted on turkey and baked ham with all the trimmings. The Red Cross provided sundry gift packages for the troops, and although they weren't much from a material standpoint, we truly appreciated the thought. Really touching was the after-dinner ceremony of singing carols by candlelight. Hell, the 17th Cavalry guys even displayed brotherhood toward us—a miracle in itself.

While absorbed in knife-throwing practice one afternoon, we once again witnessed an eye-opening incident involving an F-100 fighter jet. The guy had been approaching the Bien Hoa runway from the south for landing when we heard a muffled explosion and viewed flames with black smoke coming from the tailpipe. The jet began experiencing wild pitch-and-roll oscillations, finally stabilizing. The pilot prudently chose to eject when this occurred, experiencing routine seat separation with a good chute, and had an uneventful landing just outside the base perimeter. The jet meanwhile impacted a short distance south-west of the runway in a sickening loud crunch and colossal fire-ball. One of those weird-looking Kaman "Eggbeater" rescue choppers with the cockeyed side-by-side counter-rotating rotors was immediately dispatched to snatch the lucky pilot from what-ever gooks might have been watching. We all agreed that he most likely didn't have to buy a drink that night in their officers club during his initiation into the "Caterpillar Club" (military aircrew who've experienced emergency egress by parachute).

New Year's Eve 1967–68 went off with a drunken bang. We'd nearly exhausted our PX booze allotments through pur-chasing an ample supply of Crown Royal and Canadian Mist whiskey at the Class 6 store, and the liquor—combined with plenty of untainted beer, our pen gun distress flares, and "hand-popper" parachute illumination rockets—armed us well for the evening's celebration. The big hand finally struck twelve, and the midnight sky became a psychedelic collage of orange tracers, green, white, and red star clusters, and artillery illumination rounds. Even the enemy, located close-by outside the compound perimeter and watching every move we made, joined in the festivities with skyward-bound green tracers. In a fitting tribute to the New Year, Ranger Brubaker, well buzzed himself, screamed at the top of his lungs: "Eat, drink, and be merry, men . . . for soon we all die!"

Phuoc Vinh was located about fifty miles west-northwest of Bien Hoa. It was a known NVA/VC training and R&R center. The division commander, Major General Barsanti, selected this Michelin rubber plantation to be his LRP Company's locale for its baptism of fire, and we packed once again for the short trip.

In eager anticipation of our upcoming ultimate test, we departed Bien Hoa in C-123 aircraft for Phuoc Vinh during the late afternoon of January 2. The compound was immense in its own right and was home to the 501st Airborne Infantry, with whom we'd supposedly draw our first real enemy blood alongside one of their line platoons. It was no state secret that relations between the 501st and the LRPs had been severely strained since our last night in the World at the 2nd Brigade enlisted men's club. They had us made for holier-than-thou prima donnas, while we pegged them for low-class, low-intellect potheads and dummies.

John Renear and I decided to take a short tour of the area the day after our arrival. As with every location we had seen in Vietnam up to this point, the dividing line between the haves and have-nots was stunningly obvious. The poor villagers lived in wretched poverty, while the typical military, government, or Michelin big-shots luxuriated in air-conditioned French-style mansions and drove those ugly French Citroen sedans with the bizarre looking roof "bug-eye" taillights. What seemed to be an inexhaustible entourage of kids peddled oriental noodle packets and bottled Cokes, and with a month in-country, we had already learned a number of the absolute don'ts, such as *never* consume a bottled beverage provided by an indigenous source. More likely than not, some industrious VC or enemy sympathizer had jimmied the contents with glass shards, battery acid, rat poison, fecal matter, or whatever else they could find.

January 4 blossomed bright and cheerful, with the unmistakable staccato reports of light-weapons skirmishes in the distance. Intending to pump us up for the day's activities, Captain Fitts herded the company together for a pep talk: "Okay, men. Today is where the Michelin rubber meets the road in your training! There's about a 99.99 percent chance that we're gonna run into some pissed-off gooks today, and I don't want to see or hear about any John Wayne stuff from any of you. If you engage a gook, use well-aimed single shots, or if the situation calls for more firepower, restrict your output to accurate three-round bursts. None of this Vic Morrow *Combat!* full go-go horseshit with your weapon muzzle taking the skyward grand tour. Lastly, listen to your team leaders, and let's kick some serious ass on these motherfuckers! Good luck!" Captain Fitts's brief morale boost had been just what we needed, and it suddenly hit me that I was getting ready to go out and very possibly kill somebody and enjoying every second of it.

We and the gooks had mutual knowledge of one another's presence in the Phuoc Vinh area, so no pretense was made at employing our unit in a LRP capacity. With a line infantry platoon from the 501st taking point, we departed the compound on what was hilariously called a trail in a single file. Hell, the thing looked more like an interstate back in the World. The 501st guys seemed to take this infiltration method in stride, but I detected expressions of apprehension in our people, not least in myself. With an approximately twenty-five-meter clear space on either flank bordered by densely planted rubber trees and vegetation, we were pretty much sitting ducks for a gook ambush. This violated every dictum in our Recondo School training concerning cover and concealment.

Penetrating the plantation ever farther, we encountered numerous NVA/VC training aid boards surprisingly similar to those we'd come to know so well in our own service schools and training classes: Chicom Claymore components, AK-47 and RPD light machine-gun breakdown, antipersonnel and antitank mines, the works—all in Vietnamese. One poster that captured our attention was a painted caricature of a Caucasian soldier in tiger-fatigue uniform and camouflage face paint. Ranger Brubaker humorously translated its caption, which read: "Beware of American Long Range Patrols." Re-emphasizing what we'd learned in training, he also reminded us not to touch anything. If any of us had harbored any doubts about the reality of the situation up to this point, this gook R&R center and its associated training aids had effectively nixed them.

About forty minutes had elapsed since our departure when sporadic semi-automatic and automatic fire erupted to our front-left and right flanks. The fire increased in crescendo, working its way down the column, and I instinctively spun right to cover my area of responsibility. Little glowing green balls greeted me. Although only an extremely dangerous optical illusion, it appeared as if one could merely reach out and catch a tracer in mid-flight. Sergeant Caughorn yelled: "Walker, get the hell down! You're getting shot at, dummy!"

An enemy soldier sprang out of the brush approximately ten meters to my left front, paralleling our flank toward the rear and firing wildly from his AK-47. I stood up and took a lead on the gook, emptying a magazine on full auto, and he appeared to go down.

Jim screamed: "Goddamn, Dave, I think you tagged him!"

Just to be sure, I yelled, "Frag out!" as I tossed an M-26 grenade where I'd seen the gook drop. I changed magazines and started to move toward the gook when Sergeant Caughorn angrily shouted, "Goddamnit, Walker, stay the fuck where you're at and get down! You're gonna get fired up by our own guys!"

Willy and I simultaneously observed three more enemy firing wildly on the run while parallel to our line. They then broke off away from us, and we engaged them with well-aimed semi-auto shots. One went down at about fifty meters while the others disappeared into the brush.

As quickly as our team's first real firefight had begun, it ended. Sergeant Caughorn displayed genuine concern during his lacing down for my potentially disastrous move to check out the gook. "Walker, the gooks think we're all seven feet tall and tend to aim high, but don't push it by standing up in a contact unless there's no choice! And don't you ever again make a move for a kill zone during an active exchange of fire unless you're in a last-ditch assault!" I almost asked Sergeant Caughorn that considering we'd experienced a period of inactivity, would it be permissible for Jim and me to check for our hopeful kills? I wanted something to show—a weapon, pistol belt, pith helmet, anything to flash in front of our guys.

During the lull in action, Willy and I discussed this, our bonafide baptism under fire. We had all heard the phrase "fog of war," and the best way to describe it in my case was being in a totally focused and hyper-vigilant state of awareness. I recalled my visual field narrowing and had experienced an almost uncontrollable urge to piss my pants. Time had also seemed to slow down, especially when we'd engaged the gooks. Fear hadn't yet entered the equation, but Sergeant Caughorn assured us that when we'd had time to absorb it all, a dose of the shakes would be completely normal and acceptable. At this point, Willy and I agreed that we had just experienced the ultimate adrenaline rush. As for the second gook, he and I had no way of knowing for sure which one of us had dropped him, so we agreed to a macabre fifty-fifty split.

The break in action had induced an M-79 man from the 501st to take target practice on a coconut tree. All he received for his trouble were some small facial wounds from fragments from his own round and loud cheers from all of us. That this place bred insanity was becoming crystal clear. Where else could a young kid get away with this kind of shit?

We'd just resumed our movement forward when what seemed to be the whole world erupted in gunfire and explosions. An increasingly intense volume of the funny little green things was coming our way, as well as what Sergeant Caughorn loudly identified as 82-millimeter mortar impacts. I was in a half crouch, attempting to better scan my area and having a genuine ball firing up my area of responsibility, when from out of nowhere what felt like a Louisville Slugger whacked the left side of my face, accompanied by a loud ringing in my ears. Dizzy and totally disoriented, I fell limply to the ground, landing on my back, and through the haze and unbelievable noise, I heard Willy yelling that I'd been hit. Funny things go through one's mind during periods of high stress, and as desperate as the circumstances were, I remember saying to myself that this must be what "being knocked for a loop" and "Excedrin Headache No. 1" actually meant.

I lost consciousness for what must have been a matter of only mere seconds, reawakening to green tracers flying over me. Still on my back, I groggily retrieved my weapon and blindly returned fire where I hoped the green things were originating. The ejected hot brass from my weapon struck my neck and dropped into my open fatigue shirt collar. Still on my backside, I hastily chucked a frag in the direction I'd been firing, frantically shielding the top of my head and face afterward. The frag must not have flown very far because I received a faceful of kicked-up red clay dirt and a booster shot to my already loudly ringing ears. Markedly more powerful detonations began impacting farther to our front, which turned out to be 105-millimeter artillery support from the Phuoc Vinh battery. This ran most of the gooks off, and everything was relatively silent again, save an occasional weapons exchange or pitched grenade.

Jim Fleck, Sergeant Caughorn, and Ranger Brown were on me within seconds, and despite their jokes, it was obvious in their eyes that things weren't so hot. The piece of gook 82-millimeter mortar shrapnel that hit me had impacted just below my left eye at the top of the cheekbone, embedding itself about three quarters of an inch in my face. I had minimal light perception in the left eye, and although the right seemed to have retained normal acuity, the sunlight hurt like hell. Glenn Martinez, my homeboy from Stockton, had meanwhile been under the impression that I'd been shot, and I woozily observed him trolling the area for my nonexistent shooter. What a way to gain notoriety: I was the first combat casualty of F/58 LRP.

Ranger Brown immediately contacted Long Binh for a medevac chopper, and as he and Jim carried me to a nearby makeshift landing zone, shock finally took its hold as I barfed up the beef and rice LRP ration I'd consumed earlier. I weakly apologized to both of my rescuers, to which Ranger Brown responded that they'd get payback when I was released from the hospital. Amazingly, after all that had just gone down, I still lacked the common sense to be scared; instead, I was highly pissed off, with a matching headache.

Occasional light-weapons exchanges and grenade detonations rang out as I detected the staccato beat of the inbound dustoff bird's rotor blades. Jim Fleck filled out a manila luggage tag looking affair with "No morphine / Head wound" printed on it and attached it to my shirt lapel buttonhole. As the Huey got closer, it seemed as if the throbbing in my head was trying to match the beats of the rotor blades, and I once again attempted to set a new world record for the volume of upchuck expelled during a single episode.

The chopper touched down, and Ranger Brown and Jim Fleck literally whisked me into the awaiting arms of the onboard medic. The SP5 medic angrily pointed at my web gear, giving a cut hand signal across his throat, and Jim removed my harness. Ranger Brown patted me on the leg with a thumbs-up, and the aircraft pulled pitch for the evac hospital.

Combined with the shrill high-frequency whine of the main rotor transmission just inches above my face, and the stroboscopic effect of the main rotor blade shadows whipping through the windscreen and overhead cockpit observation blisters, I was ready to scream with the pain and disorientation they produced. The sickening metallic taste of blood draining from my eye and nasal wound had my gut turning flip-flops. The pilot's and copilot's facial expressions reflected as much concern as the medic's, and for the first time it crossed my mind that just maybe I wouldn't be walking away from this deal. I wasn't exactly afraid, more like extremely aware of my predicament and curious of what death might be like. The pilot also had concerns for the aircraft's survival as he initially hugged the deck and jinked out of the contact area. Even in my altered state, I noted with some dread that the aircraft possessed zero defensive capability other than a last-ditch *kamikaze* run on the gooks. The maneuvering brought up the little that remained of my beef stew LRP ration, which the medic took in stride with a reassuring grin. Despite the pain, nausea, and fear, uppermost in my thoughts was a desperate need to know if any of the other guys had been hit or even killed. As for my folks, I sure as hell hoped that an army sedan containing the survivor assistance officer wouldn't be pulling up to our house in the near future.

We touched down at the 24th Evacuation Hospital in Long Binh, where two medics and a Catholic chaplain awaited me with a gurney. In a well-meaning gesture, the chaplain inquired as to whether I desired being administered last rites. Well, this hadn't been one of my better days, and I spitefully told the chaplain that first off, I was a Protestant, and second, I had no plans for growing angel wings or stoking hell's fires in the near future.

—•— ⫞◊⫞ —•—

The dark emergency room with its frigid air conditioning was an utter shock to my body—and heaven-sent relief to my good eye. A beautiful young blonde nurse armed with a large pair of scissors nervously greeted me: "David, just lie still while I cut your boots and clothes off." I wasn't about to allow her to trash my uniform, considering I'd need it when I returned to the company. Amidst screams and moans from a couple of other new patients, I resolutely sat up, untied my bootlaces, undid my belt and fly, and passed out.

I was next aware of being naked on an ice-cold operating table in an even colder operating room, and the bright over-head lights really played hell on my still-splitting headache. Dr. Weiner identified himself, stating that I'd sustained fairly sub-stantial damage to my left orbital region and upper cheekbone and that he'd be grafting a small amount of skin from my outer left forehead to replace that lost in the shrapnel impact. The bone structure immediately below and outer of my left eye had been totally shattered, and Dr. Weiner humorously remarked that he'd be doing his best bondo and bailing-wire job on me. Instinctively sensing that this man meant only to do me well, I groggily requested that he not slip with the knife, thus trans-forming me into Frankenstein's monster. The OR nurse con-nected the sedative IV, Dr. Weiner instructed me to count down from 100, and I was in nowhere land by around 97.

Having lost all sense of time, I awakened to a disorienting world of pain, darkness, and muted explosions in the far distance. The unnerving sensation could well have been likened to one's having been transported to a netherworld of death, despair, and terror. I hazily recalled being hit, but when? Today? Yesterday? Three days ago? I immediately deduced that I was in a hospital bed and felt around my immediate environment, discovering a thick bandage covering my head from mid-face up and several IVs inserted in my hands and arms. Muted moans and an occasional scream of "I'm blind!" or "I want my mother!" emanated from my fellow patients, and to my own blind query of what day and time it was, an attractive-sounding female voice reassuringly answered: "Good morning, David. I'm Lieutenant Perry, the maxillofacial ward duty nurse, but you can call me Cheryl, and it's 0600 hours on the fifth of January. You've been out since about 1500 hours yesterday afternoon. You had a pretty close call out there, but Dr. Weiner performed his usual first-class body and fender work, and he'll be here in a while to tell you more. Your unit commander, Captain Fitts, also called earlier to ask how you're doing, and he relayed a message from your sergeants, Caughorn and Brown, who both order you not to get soft in here."

I heard screaming from a nearby building in what sounded to be Vietnamese, and Cheryl must have read my mind: "Don't get excited, David. It's the POW ward."

I finally mustered up the courage to ask Cheryl if I was blind, and her response was a gift from the gods of war. "No, David. Dr. Weiner has your right eye covered to prevent sympathetic reaction from your left eye.

"Okay, ma'am. Guess that's a start in the right direction."

Dr. Weiner's session of ward rounds finally made it to my bed, and he turned out to be a very personable guy. My first concerns, of course, were finding out exactly what damage had occurred to my left eye, how disfiguring the impact wound had been, and when in the hell I would be getting cut loose from this place. He didn't attempt pulling any snow job, stating that my left eye had sustained massive internal hemorrhaging and that the name of the game at this point was to just wait for a hoped-for improvement or, on the downside, watch for aggravating factors such as unchecked bleeding or dangerous clotting. A worst-case scenario would be removal of the eye and replacement with a "prosthetic appliance" should the condition worsen beyond medical capability.

As for the facial damage, Captain Weiner explained that he'd performed minor nasal repair and major cosmetic surgery, having literally reconstructed my upper left cheekbone and lower eye socket with epoxy and surgical steel wire, finishing the job with a skin graft from my forehead. "David, the scars are going to look pretty unsightly initially, but they will for the most part fade away with time. I like to call them badges of honor. To keep this all in the proper perspective, I also want you to realize that had the fragment struck an eighth of an inch higher, you would most likely be dead or at the very least severely brain damaged."

During that first day on the ward, I felt as if I were in *The Twilight Zone*. The screams were really starting to get on my nerves, and I retreated into my own little protective cocoon. No doubt because of the pain medication, I experienced bizarre dreams of waking up on the ward with my left eye completely healed, informing the nurse that my bed could be awarded to a worthy customer and to kindly provide me a lift back to my unit. The stark reality of the situation viciously returned when I'd awaken to a still screwed-up left eye and throbbing headache.

My mind wandered to other unknowns, such as what Dad and Mom would think of my battle wounds. And if I ultimately lost the eye, I knew that I could still drive a car, but I depressingly guessed that I could write off an Army career and, worse yet, flying an airplane. I also wondered if the folks had been notified of my little mishap.

The moment of truth came a couple of days later. Cheryl advised me that Dr. Weiner would be removing the head and right eye bandages, and I couldn't resist asking if she looked as good as she sounded. "I'll let you be the judge of that, David, although I've never had any complaints from the peanut gallery." This upbeat conversation had been all well and good, but a tinge of fear lingered in the back of my mind: what if my right eye had also decided to take a vacation? I sure as hell couldn't visualize myself sitting on a street corner selling VFW poppies to antiwar hippies.

Cheryl made it a point to be on hand for moral support during the unveiling, and as the layers were removed, I began perceiving normal light in the right eye. The final layer disappeared, and to my immense joy and relief, I was back in the world of the seeing. My head and mouth still ached like Babe Ruth had belted it for a home run, and the right eye was still moderately light sensitive despite the darkened ward lighting, but the old vision was still there. Dr. Weiner had a totally unexpected surprise for me. Reaching into his coat pocket, he withdrew a small wrapped box complete with bow. "David, I've made it a custom around here to give my patients lasting souvenirs of their stay in the 24th Evac. Here's the piece of Mack truck that laid you out the other day." I weakly opened the box and found the ugliest and most jagged chunk of junkyard metal I'd ever seen. "Now you'll have something to show to your kids and grandkids someday," he quipped.

With my recovered eyesight, the view of other less fortunate patients on the ward was a real downer. One guy's face had been literally blown off along with a major portion of his brain; his legs had been amputated just above the knees. All he could do was lay there whimpering incoherently in his own private hell, and I wondered whether he had a girlfriend or was married. Just to look at the guy elicited not only sympathy, but outright fear; I never had the nerve to ask Cheryl how he'd been messed up. A few mornings later, I awakened to see his bed vacant. Tragically, the poor soldier had died during the night, and he was the first of four patients who would expire during my stay on the ward. As Cheryl gently explained it, post-op infection was the big killer in Vietnam hospitals. Almost unbelievably, this was minor in comparison to what I'd witness during the next twenty months.

Both Cheryl and Dr. Weiner had virtually ordered me to write Dad and Mom as soon as I was physically capable, telling me that the War Office had sent a telegram informing them of my having been "moderately wounded." I was still unable to sit up for more than a few seconds without feeling faint, and I scribbled out a short note while lying on my back. As for the telegram, all I could imagine was Mom's totally freaking out. (I was right.)

In what would become an every-other-day routine, good old Staff Sergeant Hutchinson showed up with gifts for his way-laid troop. The two sixteen-ounce cans of Pabst Blue Ribbon he smuggled in were a godsend, but the rock-hard Hershey's Tropical Chocolate bars with rubber peanuts were useless to me, although I never let on. Hutch further stated that big trouble was brewing with an impending gook offensive and that the U.S. Marine Corps "combat loss" M-14 that he was giving me could prove to be beneficial. He'd broken it down into the two basic groups and camouflaged it in a laundry bag along with three full mags and a few boxes of ammo. "Just hide it in plain sight next to your nightstand." If anything went down, my first destination would be the next-door POW ward.

Hutch brought me up to speed on the latest gossip and other info. To my immense relief, nobody else—other than the 501st M-79 hotshot—had been injured in the rubber plantation, and the company had just moved north to Song Be for a major operation. Captain Fitts and Top Walker would be in to check up on me in a day or two. Hutch hinted that Captain Fitts had something for me, but try as I did to extract the information—what could it be? an Article 15? a promotion? a chewing out?—he wouldn't give it up.

Just like clockwork, Hutch strutted into the ward two days later with Captain Fitts and Top Walker. I was still pretty weak and sore but managed to sit up in what I thought to be at least a semblance of the position of attention. Captain Fitts shook my hand as he handed me a manila envelope, and Top removed a folded sheet from his fatigue shirt pocket. "Attention to orders, Department of the Army, Headquarters, 101st Airborne Division, APO San Francisco 96383. The following award is announced—" I was in an emotional blur as Top read the special order awarding me the Combat Infantry Badge, and Captain Fitts pinned the badge on my pajama shirt. All three of my superiors made a really big show of the presentation, and Cheryl even jumped in on the action.

In a further effort to bolster my spirits, Captain Fitts relayed that all of the guys in the company were pulling for me and that I was to quit ghosting and get my young ass back to work as soon as possible. As my trio of superiors prepared to depart, I requested that Captain Fitts relay my boundless thanks to Ranger Brown, Jim Fleck, Sergeant Caughorn, and the chopper aircrew who'd pulled my boob out of the wringer a few days prior.

I'd been hospitalized for around two weeks when Dr. Weiner decided to inspect my left eye. The remaining bandages and gauze came off, and objects on the ward were clear in the right eye, but although the ward was well lit, the end effect through my left eye was akin to being in a dark room. Dr. Weiner was straight up with his evaluation, explaining that he was unhappy with the lack of progress in the reduction of internal bleeding, and if things didn't stabilize in the near future, the eye would become diseased and begin atrophying. If things got worse, I'd be sent to Japan. Call it extrasensory perception or whatever, but I knew then and there that I was on borrowed time in uniform, and the prospect sent shivers down my spine. Getting shuffled off to Japan nearly always guaranteed a trip back to the states and a medical discharge in circumstances such as mine, and my gears began spinning in devising a plan to thwart this fate.

Cheryl passed the word a few mornings later that Major General Barsanti, the 101st Airborne Division's commander, would be making an awards presentation appearance for a number of patients in the afternoon, and she suggested that those of us physically able tidy up a bit. The general personally awarded me the Purple Heart, which caught me totally by surprise. Prior to departing my bedside, he asked whether I needed anything, and I jumped at the opportunity: "Well, sir, the doc informs me that there's a better-than-average chance that I'll be going back to the World for a medical separation, and I sure wouldn't mind receiving a promotion to sergeant." The general briefly questioned me about time in grade and service, efficiency reports, and other things, and gave me a dated handwritten note, countersigned by his aid, that said I was promoted to sergeant, effective immediately.

After three weeks in a bed, it was a relief to finally be granted restricted ambulatory privileges. Now I could not only take (initially very unsteady) short walks on the hospital compound and rebuild my strength, but most importantly, I could ditch the bed pan for calls of nature; I'd despised it since being admitted.

Dr. Weiner had arranged that I be detailed to physical therapy, a charitable term for "make work," and asked me about any unique skills I might possess, other than trained assassin. The first thing I thought of was my administrative skills, and I was assigned to the hospital administration office for two hours a day, mostly doing rote clerical work such as typing and stamping generic information on various forms. This position would truly have its advantages in the near future, or so I thought.

By the latter part of the month, I'd regained sufficient strength and stamina to be transferred to the full ambulatory ward—a necessity from the hospital staff's perspective, considering the ever-increasing flood of new customers. Unlike Cheryl's ward, this place was run like a gulag by a male nurse, Captain Long.

The move coincided with a visit from Captain Fitts and Top Walker, who, although glad to see me, also bore very bad news. The company had been involved in a major engagement in the Song Be area on January 23, and Sgt. Joe Griffis and SP4 John McChesney had been KIA from an 82-millimeter mortar impact. As Top described it, McChesney had been literally vaporized by a direct hit. SP4 John Gentile had been seriously wounded in his arms and chest during the same action and was now just a few doors away on the ICU. To my recollection, I'd never made Griffis's acquaintance, but McChesney and Gentile were close friends.

Captain Fitts requested that I accompany him and Top for a visit with Gentile, and what we encountered was a young man overcome by fear and pain. As I approached his bedside, John feebly reached for my hand as he broke into tears. I was at a loss for words and gently held John's mangled right hand in an effort to comfort him. I thought about our Recondo School training and how gung-ho we'd all been for the big test. Frankly, I was totally overwhelmed by how quickly these life-changing experiences had occurred not only with me, but our other guys as well. Being a top-priority patient, John was quickly evacuated to Japan, and I never saw him again.

As Captain Fitts and Top prepared to head back to work, I casually mentioned the recent on-the-spot promotion by Major General Barsanti and that I hadn't received the orders. Their mutual reassurance that the matter would be resolved pacified me for the time being.

The Tet Offensive was officially launched on January 31, and the hospital had several day and night red alerts with air-raid sirens, panicking medical personnel, heavy helicopter activity, the whole bit. In actuality, enemy forces never achieved close proximity to the Long Binh complex, and although artillery detonations and small arms were clearly audible in the distance, our safety was never an issue.

A steady stream of letters had been arriving from my folks, most of which remained unanswered on my part. It wasn't that I was being intentionally cruel, but what in the hell was there to say? A lot had happened to me in an extremely compressed time period, and it was enough of an effort just keeping myself focused and avoiding the trap of depression. I'd get this sorted out in my own time and way, then deal with domestic issues.

The news I'd been dreading from Dr. Weiner finally came. The left eye was doing poorly, and I'd be sent to Japan shortly for more definitive care. As always, he was straight to the point, making an educated guess that I'd be further transferred to a stateside hospital with facilities specializing in ophthalmic injuries, probably in Denver.

But I had a plan to escape this nightmare, and it was time to put it into action. At this point, I'd acquired a working knowledge of the various hospital forms and had long since been familiarized with the phrase "creative paper work" through Rick Carmen at the Wiesbaden Airborne School. In short order, I had a doctor's release-for-duty form in hand, complete with "No Duty Assignment Limitations" and Dr. Weiner's signature stamp.

My uniform and sunglasses had been stored in the hospital supply room and were available on demand. Much to my relief, the megabuck Heuer watch that I'd received from Dad as a Christmas present in 1965 was present and undamaged. I covertly grabbed the few possessions I had on the ward, including Hutch's M-14, and made a dash to pick up my clothes. The supply NCO returned them with no questions asked, and with my freshly produced paperwork, all it took was a quick change in a linen closet to transform me into a discharged hospital patient. The shades would aid in camouflaging my wounds, I smugly reassured myself.

I asked the supply sergeant for directions to Camp Ray, and he cheerfully stated that I had no need for this; his clerk would drive me right smack to the company area.

I'd really outsmarted myself on this deal as the trip to Camp Ray was a torture session. Removing Dr. Weiner's metal eye shield and gauze patch prior to visiting the company area had been a serious mistake, and the road dust really irritated the bad eye. By the time we arrived at the LRP compound, my head was throbbing at about the same level of intensity as when

I'd been hit, and the right eye was reacting with unabated tearing and involuntary squinting. As if that weren't enough, the slowly healing damage to my nose stung like hell and had me constantly on the verge of sneezing, further aggravating the headache.

The company area was a virtual ghost town. I entered our team hooch, and almost everything appeared to be just as it had been prior to our departing for Phuoc Vinh, save my now missing bedding and footlocker. I dizzily stumbled to the supply room, and there sat Hutch at his desk, his jaw agape over my unannounced appearance. "Dave, what in the hell are you doing here? The medics informed us that you're probably headed for Japan." I handed the doctor's release to Hutch, and he chuckled while flat-out asking me if I'd been its author. "I know that you've been working in the hospital admin office, and all I have to do is take one look to know that you haven't been returned to duty. You're white as a sheet, and your left eye is draining pus like a Saigon whore's twat!"

My heart sank as Hutch tore up the masterpiece I'd created and tossed the remains in File 13. Well, the master plan ruse was up before it had really begun, and Hutch handed me a duffle bag containing my personal gear. I advised Hutch that his M-14 was still in my possession, and he directed me to keep it. Should I in fact be evacuated out of country, I was to transfer it to a trusted ward medic.

Hutch's jeep ride back to the hospital was a total letdown. I'd convinced myself that the escape plan was foolproof, and he'd made me right from the get-go. I guess the hospital wristband that I'd stupidly neglected to remove had been a dead giveaway, too. No doubt sensing that I already felt sufficiently crummy, Hutch chose to counsel rather than reprimand. "Dave, I know you want to get back with the guys, but you need to realize that in your present condition, you'd be a hazard not only to yourself, but also the team on a mission." Back once again at the hospital, Hutch wished me luck with his sincere hope that I get the physical problem fixed and return to the company.

Defeat and frustration temporarily overrode my steely resolve as Hutch sped off for Camp Ray, and I experienced my first good bawling episode since that day on the Fort Ord rifle range. Why couldn't these medics just put me on light duty in the company until I healed up?

Thoughtfully, Hutch had included my issue of Vietnamese tiger-stripe uniforms, survival knife, strobe light, poncho liners, and web gear (minus ordnance) with my personal stuff. At least these artifacts provided something tangible to connect me with the company.

The morning of February 28 began with the always unwelcome early wakeup call and the announcement that I'd be leaving for Japan in two hours. The mood in Dr. Weiner's office was subdued. "David, our care facilities here are simply insufficient for the demands of your case. Right now, our primary concerns are eliminating the present infection and preventing its recurrence, which in this bacteria-ridden environment is totally futile." Over the course of our doctor-patient relationship, we had shared similar viewpoints on various subjects, and as we shook hands in parting, Dr. Weiner's final order was "When you get home, give the hippies hell for your ol' doc."

The farewell with Cheryl was emotional. This fine lady and nurse had coaxed me back to relative health and raised my spirits when down. I owed this wonderful girl a lot, and as a small token of affection, I presented her with a 101st Recondo brand. In response, she gave me a hug and kiss on the cheek. As I departed Cheryl's ward, I surrendered Hutch's M-14 to her male medical technician. (As I eventually found out, I could have taken the thing home as our bags were never inspected.)

About twenty of us were packed on a bus bound for Bien Hoa. Along with patients from other area evac hospitals, we'd be boarding a MAC C-141 bound for Yokota, Japan, about twenty-five miles northwest of Tokyo. I had been in Vietnam eighty-seven days.

Team 2-1, F/58 LRP, Bien Hoa, December 1967. Standing, left to right: Caughorn, author, Fleck, Sachs. Kneeling: Wilson.

The author's fifteenth day with 5th Platoon (author circled).

The author's sixth day in the army, July 19, 1965.

Harry Walker (left) and author in BCT PX stockade, July 1965.

Blackening our M-14 sights on Fort Ord BRM range, September 1965 (arrow points to author).

Author as part of the 8th Infantry Division Airborne
School cadre, Wiesbaden AB, Germany, February 1967.

Drill Sergeant Vibbard.

Assistant Drill Sergeant
Burton.

Author on N/75 rappelling tower, November 1970.

Team Hotel, N/75 Ranger. Left to right: Wooley, Blow, author, Lyons, Ramsland, and Kirk.

Hotel Team Kit Carson scout Hai.

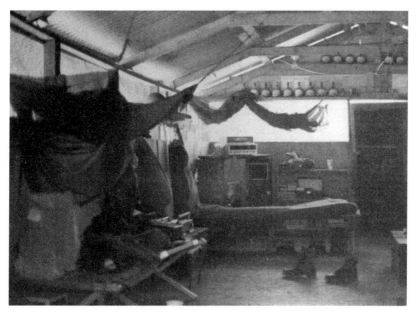

Hotel Team hooch.

Team Hotel Christmas tree, 1970.

Team Hotel in Fish Hook, January 1971. Hai and Kirk are in foreground; arrow points to author.

Phil Tischman (center) drawing down on author in Hotel hooch. Jake Dymond (foreground) and Stephen Joley (right).

Author (foreground) and Chuck Lyons in Soui Ca, January 1971.

Sandbag detail, N/75 Ranger.

N/75 beret award formation, March 1971.

N/75 Ranger orderly room sign.

N/75 Ranger gate sign.

Remnants of N/75 Ranger Club following Typhoon Wanda, April 1971.

Heavy N/75 team awaiting infil bird (arrow points to author).

Dave Blow (left) and author hiding from Top Moore, April 1971.

Heavy N/75 team awaiting infil bird (arrow points to author).

Author in Fish Hook, May 1971.

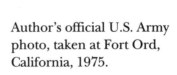

Author's official U.S. Army photo, taken at Fort Ord, California, 1975.

Left to right: Kirk, Blow, and author (arrow) in Soui Ca.

Chuck Lyons (right background) soaking author during Soui Ca "heavy" mission, April 1971.

Team Hotel infilled in Nui Mieus, April 1971.

The author's early
LRP mentor and
friend, Capt. Roger
B. "Hog" Brown.

Leroy "Jake" Dymond (left) and Joseph D. "Jay" Hayes about one hour prior to Hayes being KIA in Nui Mieu Mountains, June 13 1971.

Jay Hayes KIA memorial service, June 14, 1971.

Recon Platoon, 3/21 IN 196 LIB, January 1972 (author is in back row, far left).

3/21 Recon Platoon buddies. Left to right: author, Cummings (seated), Whisler, and Davenport.

The author's BE-18T freighter, in the vicinity of Donner Summit, California, 1989. PHOTO COURTESY OF MARK EVANS, UNION FLIGHTS, INC.

Left to right: author's wife, Chris; his son-in-law, Kenn; daughter, Allison; and author, 1993.

Author's father, George E. Walker, January 1942.

CHAPTER 6

Hospital to Hospital

249TH GENERAL HOSPITAL, FEBRUARY TO MARCH 1968

The Air Force flight crew members had their own emotional defense methods for coping with carnage and jokingly referred to our medevac aircraft as the "airborne meat wagon." The stretcher patients were boarded before the ambulatory types, and considering their various states of disrepair, I then fully realized just how relatively lucky I'd been.

The flight to Yokota passed rapidly. To their immense credit, the Air Force flight nurses adhered to a manic workload of administering medications, maintaining close monitoring of the critical cases, and comforting the occasional whiner. An extremely critical stretcher patient died en route, and his young nurse broke down in tears. All that mattered to me was the stark fact of being back in a C-141 headed in what for me was the wrong direction, all of my plans tossed in the trash can and Vietnam already seeming like a dream.

The deplaning at Yokota was a total shocker. We had departed a tropical climate mere hours earlier, only to encounter freezing temperatures and fresh snow. I'd always thought the whole country was hot and humid like Vietnam. The Air Force head nurse explained to us that the Tet Offensive had created a mass overflow of patients and that we'd be spending at least one night in the base hospital before transferring to respective service facilities. In some cases, depending on severity of wounds, illness, or bed availability, a patient might be assigned to a hospital not run by his parent service. I recalled a conversation with Dr. Weiner in which he mentioned the 249th General Hospital, which was suitably staffed and equipped for my condition.

We were assigned wards according to nature of wounds, and I became acquainted with an individual who would ultimately share the entire hospital experience with me. Sgt. Jim Hawkins was a line doggie from the 501st Infantry who had incurred a wound virtually identical to mine in his right eye, also suffering the indignity of taking an AK-47 slug in his gut.

The ten-minute chopper ride to Camp Drake (Asaka) and the 249th General Hospital the next morning was picturesque, with Mount Fujiyama clearly in view. Jim and I were assigned to Ward 5, an outlying single-story building with a beautiful view of Fujiyama. Capt. Bill Sanford was the supervising ward nurse, and 2nd Lt. Nancy Still, a perky early-20s brunette from Portland, Oregon, actually ran the place. Captain Sanford was a very personable type of guy who closely resembled Fred Gwynne (a/k/a Herman Munster) in physical appearance and demeanor. Being a fairly relaxed type, he preferred being addressed as Cappy rather than sir. As for Lieutenant Still, herself a total sweetheart just like Cheryl, Nancy or Ms. Still worked just fine.

The ward had a TV that received broadcasts from a couple of the local Tokyo channels and AFTV (as in Europe). We all busted our guts watching episodes of *The Lone Ranger* dubbed in Japanese. AFTV naturally ran programs in English, and the unanimous favorite of the combat veteran patients was, naturally, *Combat.*

The first consultation with my new doctor, Major Strassman, was disappointing. He darkened the room and switched on a standard eye test chart, asking me what I could see through the bad eye. Other than a blur of dim light, I couldn't see anything. He placed a plastic disc with a small round hole over my left eye, and I was able to discern the second-from-bottom line darkly. Ironically, the brief glimpse of the eye chart during that initial exam was the last time the left eye would see anything at all, and several subsequent appointments with Dr. Strassman showed only a downward trend with the internal bleeding.

The hospital had a PACEX drycleaners/alterations conces-
sion, and I took advantage of the skilled Japanese lady's fabri-
cating subdued and non-subdued F/58 LRP scrolls. I hadn't yet
totally tossed in the towel for remaining on active duty, and the
scrolls would be a real attention-getter in my next duty assignment, or so I optimistically believed.

Steve Anderson was a Navy petty officer first class and recent
divorcee (from a Japanese wife) who had suffered second-
degree steam burns to his face and hands aboard ship, seriously
scalding the areas surrounding his eyes. His vision, thankfully,
was unharmed, but the resultant infections from scalding had
wound him up on our ward. As a sailor, Steve naturally possessed total familiarity with not only nearby Yokosuka Naval
Base, but also Tokyo. According to Steve, if our ragtag crew of
Jim and me accompanied him on a day pass, we would experience the luxury of first-class prime rib, steak, lobster, or whatever else our ravenous hearts desired in the Yokosuka Navy
Base's Chief Petty Officer Club. And we might even be able to
squeeze in a quick look-see at nearby Tokyo. So, just like in the
Jap monster movies, our threesome of tourist adventurers
boarded a commuter train to Yokosuka Naval Base.

The base was an immense sprawling area with high activity
and many docked ships, and the CPO club was an elegant three-
story building designed to resemble a large pagoda. The atmosphere within was cordial, although I sensed an air of curiosity in
the senior NCOs. I guess Army personnel were a seldom-seen
entity, and the F/58 LRP scroll on my summer greens definitely
drew some double-takes. The food was better than Steve had
claimed, and I attacked a medium-rare sixteen-ounce sirloin
steak and fries with total abandon. On the other hand, Jim and
Steve had the biggest slices of medium-rare end-cut prime rib
I'd ever seen. If I'd thought that San Francisco and Los Angeles
had a lot of neon lights, Tokyo set a new standard. Altogether,
our little junket was well worth the time spent, and we'd have
lifetime bragging rights to having seen Tokyo.

A final consultation with Dr. Strassman was the hammer's
drop. The left eye had shown zero improvement, and despite

my shameless begging to be returned to my unit in Vietnam, he solemnly compounded the misery by stating that I'd just been reassigned to the 249th Medical Holding Company for further movement to Fitzsimmons General Hospital in Denver. With the stroke of a pen, my official affiliation with F/58 LRP had been severed forever. Most disturbingly, if my condition proved to be extended or even permanent, I'd be referred to the Army's physical evaluation board for reassignment to the temporary or permanent disability retired lists for final disposition. Almost as if having been choreographed in a movie script, Jim received the same news from Dr. Strassman. We'd be shipping out for Fitzsimmons at the end of March.

Our last night in Japan was restless, and since Nancy was pulling the graveyard shift, Jim and I decided to provide her with some company on the nurse's station. As a joke, I made reference to her collar brass appearing to be slightly tarnished, and that started the party. Appearing with a can of Brasso and a baby diaper from my nightstand, we proceeded to provide Nancy with a block of instruction in proper maintenance of her insignias. My last (and loving) recollection of Nancy was overhearing her subdued sobs on the nurse's station. We'd also greatly miss Captain Sanford, who had heroically—and for the most part good-naturedly—endured our boyish stunts and general mayhem from day one.

FITZSIMMONS GENERAL HOSPITAL, MARCH TO AUGUST 1968

The C-141 departed Tachikawa Air Base at 1000 hours the next morning on an east-northeast course, and we were feet-wet over the Pacific minutes later. Our prepaid transoceanic trip would take us first to Travis Air Force Base in California and then to Lowry Air Force Base in Colorado. Probably because of the mild pain medication that I was still prescribed and the five Burgermeister beers I'd smuggled aboard the aircraft, I quickly surrendered to peaceful sleep. Before I'd had a chance to look out the window, we were over the central California coastline on vectors for Travis.

The arrival at Lowry held no surprises in terms of the weather. We had departed Japan in freezing temperature and found Travis experiencing sunny California conditions, and here we were back again frolicking in the snow. Jim remarked that if all of us patients didn't die from our wounds, the abrupt climatic changes would probably do us in. We were initially assigned to Ward 8-S in the main hospital for intake, and our room provided a bird's-eye view of East Colfax Avenue, the primary east-west thoroughfare, as well as of the suburb of South Aurora.

A call home early in the evening addressed my desperately needed contact with the folks. I knew they'd been through hell, especially in view of my inexcusable correspondence habits, and I promised to improve stateside. Ending the call to Mom's background wailing, I told Dad that I'd swing convalescent leave as soon as possible.

Our first night in Fitzsimmons had its traumas. A twenty-three-year-old Army sergeant, Ira Maxwell, had been wheeled into an adjacent room in the middle of the night, screaming and cursing at the medics and nurses over his having been blinded and wanting to die. I was travel-weary and frankly not in any frame of mind to hear this at zero-dark-thirty, and I screamed at him to shut up. Jim agreed. This earned us a severe—and well-deserved—reprimand from Capt. Sharon Warren, the graveyard shift nurse.

Sharon hadn't in the least understated Ira's condition. He had tripped a "Bouncing Betty" land mine fourteen days earlier and had lost his right leg up to the groin, including most of his family jewels. The detonation had additionally cost him the loss of his right arm to the elbow and the physical loss of both eyes, along with grotesque facial wounds. In shock and total humility, Jim and I just stared at one another. Although heavily sedated, Ira was able to engage in small talk with us later in the morning. He'd been a squad leader in a line infantry unit with the 25th Infantry Division and had just fallen short of receiving a six-month "drop" from the combat zone and "early out" from the Army.

Other than a slight decrease of internal bleeding, Maj. John Kearney, the chief staff ophthalmologist, offered little encouragement following his initial exam of the bad eye. And worse yet, as with Dr. Weiner and Dr. Strassman, his torture kit included the dreaded suction cup, hypo needle, and that god-damned bright light contraption. With the next day being my twentieth anniversary of life, I took a shot in the dark and informed the doc that I'd had enough fun, travel, and adventure being shuffled around the world for a while and just wanted to get home to my family for a break. Wishing me a happy birthday, he cheerfully granted my wish, stating that I'd be placed on thirty-day convalescent leave, effective at 0600 the next morning.

I was in a taxi to the Denver airport by 0500. Unlike San Francisco, the Denver terminal had managed to maintain normalcy and patriotism within its doors. Sure, peacenick vagrants were by now commonplace in any major U.S. transportation facility, and I'd even detected one obvious loiterer during my instinctive "bogie-swivel," but on the whole, the travelers I observed were your basic everyday hard-working "Wild West" Americans.

The reunion with Dad and Mom was bittersweet. Never in my life had I seen either of my parents so emotionally distraught, and as they hugged me, I felt their trembling. With her full attention directed at my eye shield and my few newly acquired uniform items, Mom sobbingly asked me what happened. "Well, Ma, as my teammate Jim Fleck said when I got hit, my head tried to occupy the same airspace as a chunk of gook shrapnel. The shrapnel won, but I'm really okay now." Obviously motivated to distract Mom from my wounds, Dad stated that we could all talk about that later. In the meantime, it was off to Sharpe Army Depot and my twentieth birthday party.

At the party, I met a strikingly attractive redhead named Susan O'Connor. She was one of Mom's coworkers, and Mom told me she was five months younger than me. To my immense fortune and joy, Susan had also been attracted to me, and through Mom's eager encouragement, we agreed to link up as soon as possible during my leave. Now I'd have to undo all I'd learned over the past years to treat Susan like a lady rather than a GI's Fayette-Nam bimbo pickup.

Finally arriving home later that afternoon, I felt a weight lifted off my shoulders as I embraced our little snow-white Pekingese puppy dog, Tootie, and dropped off into a peaceful slumber with her cradled in my arms—in my own bed for a change.

My '57 Chevy had astoundingly remained in one piece. I hadn't anticipated any serious problems with driving and was relieved to confirm that later in the morning. Other than having to turn my head farther left when changing lanes and being a little more conscious of obstacle clearance on the vehicle's right side, everything felt normal. And although I no longer possessed depth perception, I could perceive relative motion and make size comparisons just fine. (Apparently, I picked the correct eye to lose. If it had been the right, the California DMV would have required special multilensed, wide-angle rearview mirrors.)

To my surprise and relief, Manteca hadn't yet been totally overrun by the hippie invasion. As it had been before I'd left for Vietnam, there were a few freaks on the sidelines, but most of the young people still looked and acted relatively conservative. Nevertheless, I felt disconnected from everything and everybody not military-related. By now, I was realistic enough not to expect any positive homecoming beyond what I'd received from Mom's crew.

Army SP4 Ed Quinn, a fellow classmate from Manteca High, was also home on DEROS leave from Vietnam, where he had received the Silver Star for gallantry in action while serving with the 1st Infantry Division. He had also recently married his Manteca High girlfriend, Vicky Hart. Having by now experienced a couple of wonderful trysts with Susan, I suggested to Ed that our foursome take a tour of Stockton in his new '68 Chevelle Malibu SS 396. What neither of the women expected was Ed's and my attempt, fueled by Red Mountain wine, to violate every traffic law in downtown Stockton.

A few days before my return to Fitzsimmons, we received a letter from Gary in Germany. For openers, the little shit had graduated from Bad Tolz jump school and immediately submitted a 1049 for the 173rd Airborne in Vietnam. This revelation naturally disrupted my folk's emotional well-being and spurred my fear and anger. All I could pray for was that Gary's request for transfer would be denied or, better yet, the war would end before he got there.

I arrived back at Fitzsimmons in a cloud. I had developed the skills to effectively deal with my own problems, but the realization that I could lose my little brother had exhausted me emotionally and physically. The folks had already gone through pure hell with my being hit, and Gary's potential wounding or death would really create eternal misery in our family.

A quick check-in with Leslie was encouraging. Ira had been fitted with plastic "conformer" prosthetic eyes, sort of "training wheels" for the final prosthetics he would receive prior to discharge, and an industrious ward mate had made him a spare set of conformers in American flag and camo designs at the cccupational therapy clinic. Leslie further stated that Jim had been transferred to an outlying medical holding company ward, 502, a couple of weeks earlier, and advised me to pack up and join him.

Ward 502 was a memory-lane return to Splinter Village, and its main selling point was no morning formations or make-work stuff. By hospital policy, those physically and mentally capable were supposed to participate in occupational therapy or other duties, like the dreaded burial details. Life on the ward pretty much matched the life of Riley. We had a new Army-provided Soni Trinitron color TV on which to watch our favorite programs while scarfing down delivered fried chicken and barbecued ribs from Chicken Delight. For all practical purposes, we medical holding company patients were on paid vacations.

The status of my promotion orders had been a source of annoyance since the 24th Evacuation Hospital, and an inquiry with the hospital's adjutant general office provided no joy. I was being carried on the medical holding company rolls as a sergeant, but I wasn't receiving the pay. I was told to just be patient.

Dr. Kearney's final exam at the end of July sealed my fate in the Army. The left eye had by then become hopelessly atrophied, and I'd be medically boarded on August 7 to the temporary disability retired list pending further disposition. I therefore had eight days left in the Army.

Before I'd even realized it, separation day was upon me. I bade last-minute good-byes to Leslie, Jim, Ira, and the other guys, and then it was down to the Adjutant General's Office for final out-processing and the physical evaluation board. The final "board" turned out to be a zit-faced first lieutenant with an obviously negative attitude toward combat vets. With a smirk on his face, the lieutenant stated that it was my option to remain on active duty with a waiver, but that I'd never again serve in a combat unit or even handle weapons. The best I could hope for would be on-the-job training or attendance at a noncombat service school, such as administration. The final blow came when I had to sign the DD-214, which had "SP4-E4" in the rank/grade block. I informed the lieutenant of the error and showed him Barsanti's witnessed note. He told me to take it up with MILPERCEN in St. Louis.

I spun around without being dismissed and felt like a castaway as I angrily strutted, bag and baggage, out of the main hospital building. A saying I'd heard from Dad many years prior came to mind: "The sour and dark days behind you will seem like sweetness and light compared to the royal screwing you take today."

CHAPTER 7

Back on the Block

The one-way flight to San Francisco provided me with plenty of time to reflect. I had just been banished from my secure haven, stripped of my identity, and sent back home, where most, if not all, of my civilian friends had long since departed for whatever reasons. Not the least depressing was the issue of my now being unemployed. The monthly untaxed disability check of $269.00 would give me beer money, but the sensation that I'd come full circle was unnerving—virtually identical to that evening more than three years earlier when I'd departed home as a wet-behind-the-ears and scared-to-death kid. Of only minor consolation was the fact that I'd gypped the Army out of the remaining eleven months on my 1966 reenlistment obligation.

Dad and Mom picked me up at the airport, which had the by-then predictable scene of hippie catcalls and counterculture "dysfunction junction" atmosphere. I'd been able to ditch the eye shield shortly after the hospital leave, but even with sunglasses, the head wound scars were very prominent. A small group of war demonstrators, obviously having learned from oft-repeated experience to maintain a safe distance from their objects of scorn, couldn't resist hurling insults at me. "Hey, war hero! Looks like you got what was coming to you, huh? Too bad the Viet Cong and North Vietnamese didn't finish the job!" I had heard this crap since rotating from Germany, and it wasn't as if I'd expected anything less by then. What hurt most were the expressions of helplessness in Dad and Mom's faces.

We arrived home, and with great reluctance, I solemnly hung my khaki uniform, along with my entire young adult life up to this point, in Gary's and my bedroom closet. Technically,

113

I would remain on active duty for the next seven days, and I already felt myself to be in a state of limbo.

Over the next year and a half, I'd live with the folks rent-free and work as a United Airlines single-point aircraft refueler, an aircraft maintenance shop helper, and a drill press operator for International Harvester. I also made two abortive attempts at higher education at the local junior college and a private civil-engineering college. In both places, many—though not all—of the faculty and students were offended by, and sometimes even outright hostile toward, my jungle-fatigue shirt (my security blanket) and Vietnam-veteran status. One long-haired faculty member in the junior college even deliberately singled me out, exclaiming before the entire class that my LRP scroll labeled me as a sociopath mad-dog killer. I stormed out of the classroom, never to return.

On the plus side, a patriotic pro-servicemen Manteca auto dealer provided one hell of a deal on my first new car, a 1969 Plymouth Roadrunner in the special-order "Richard Petty Blue" paint scheme.

Gary would catch an AK-47 slug in Vietnam while serving with the 173rd Airborne Brigade, nearly losing his left leg in the process. Luckily, I'd been the one to intercept the telegram from the War Department, at least saving the folks a greater measure of heartbreak. As for me, I felt both anger and envy for his having been over there in my place. I also harbored a manic desire for revenge over his being hit.

While watching Walter Cronkite's news report one afternoon in late 1968, I saw Jim Venable wounded and bedridden in Japan. (Years later, Gary Linderer informed me that he'd been seriously wounded and Al Contreros killed on the same mission.)

In early 1969, I finally lost my degenerating left eye through surgical removal at Letterman General Hospital in San Francisco and was transferred to the permanent disability retired list. I considered this to be a genuine bummer. Shortly afterward, I developed tonsillitis and had my tonsils removed at Oak Knoll

Naval Hospital in Oakland. The tonsillectomy was more painful than having the eye yanked out.

An ill-fated gesture at membership in the local Veterans of Foreign Wars post resulted in their happily accepting my dues, only to treat me as a leper outcast afterward. As thanks for this warm welcome home, I demanded and received a refund of the dues. Not to be outdone by his son, Dad ripped up his membership card.

Old Man Fate still had his own ideas. The U.S. Army and the gooks hadn't seen the last of Dave Walker yet.

CHAPTER 8

Back in the "Green Machine"

The late-night phone call on Christmas Eve 1969 was totally unexpected. "Hi, Dave, this is Staff Sgt. Jim Grimmett with the Army Recruiting Office in Stockton. Do you still want to go back in the service?" Out of sheer reflex, I excitedly answered, "Hell yeah!" Grimmett requested a meeting the second day following New Years. My re-entry was to take place on January 9, 1970.

When we met, Jim Grimmett greeted me with open arms. "Welcome back, Dave! It took nine months of paper shuffling, but together we pulled it off!" The official DA paperwork had arrived at Jim's office during early Christmas week. It declared my eligibility for return to active duty based on a "Moral Waiver for Combat Wounded Veterans." Partially hampering my elation was the issue of rank. In typical Army fashion, the promotion to sergeant granted by Major General Barsanti in the 24th Evacuation Hospital was never processed. I'd be sworn in as an SP4 with more than four years of service for pay, but stuck with a new date of rank effective January 9, 1970. I realized that had I opted for retention on active duty and reassignment from Fitzsimmons, I could have avoided all of this crap.

With only six days left out of uniform, I faced numerous cleanup chores, not the least of which was my kid-glove handling of Dad and Mom. Gary, now stationed at Fort Ord, had only recently been released from Madigan Army Hospital at Fort Lewis for his serious combat wounds, and just when the smoke had almost cleared, here I was preparing to drag them through it all over again. Though deeply concerned, Dad shared my belief that a man had to do what his gut told him. Mom on the other hand envisioned my flag-draped coffin and

117

a twenty-one-gun salute at the Presidio of San Francisco cemetery. I tried to comfort her with the likelihood of my Army job
being restricted to a rear-echelon gig in the states or some
noncombat overseas area.

On the ninth, I jumped in the Roadrunner bound for Oakland. Jim Grimmett had strongly suggested that I report in uniform, which he guaranteed would place me at the head of the
assembly line. He was right. The physical exam and oath of
enlistment were accomplished in a flash. On the downside, the
medics had cursed me with a permanent Category 4 (P-4) vision
profile, stating "NO ASSIGNMENT TO COMBAT AREAS."
With orders in hand, I headed for Fort Ord and the Reception
Station Holding Company pending further assignment.

Passing through Fort Ord's main gate onto post was a senti-
mental and anxious experience. Pulling into the parking lot, I
recalled this very area as having been where it all began for me
on that daunting and homesick night almost four and a half
years earlier.

An amicable NCO assigned me a room, stating that other
than obtaining an active-duty ID card, drawing a new uniform
issue, and attending the mandatory Monday-through-Friday
formations at 0830, I'd be on my own for the time being. With
no bed-check concerns, point recon missions for females in
nearby Seaside and Monterey would be a breeze. Another paid
vacation!

Like a felon irresistibly drawn back to his crime scene, I
took a spin up the hill for a look at H-1-3. Virtually nothing
had changed, and the sensation was as if existing in a time
warp. Gingerly stepping into the orderly room, I disbelievingly
encountered the familiar stocky figure of now Sgt. 1st Class Bill
Vibbard. His puzzled gaze zeroed in on my plastic name plate,
and the light bulb suddenly illuminated. Since Jim Grimmett's
phone call a couple of weeks earlier, I'd been in a state of emotional limbo, viewing myself as neither civilian nor military.
Now I'd been reunited with a man whom I totally admired and
respected, and the long-dormant sense of brotherhood and

belonging I'd so dearly missed was reborn. Bill and I associated regularly until my departure for Fort Bragg.

Other than occasional details as a post stockade prisoner escort, the majority of my time during the ensuing two weeks was spent contemplating my future. Then, one fateful morning at the main post snack bar, who should stroll in but Master Sergeant Harris, the post's Special Forces liaison and procurement NCO. Zeroing in on my F/58 LRP scroll and 101st Recondo brand, he asked to join me. Having provided him a brief rundown of my prior service and present status, he came right to the point: "Walker, how would like to join Special Forces? Mrs. Alexander and I are pretty tight, and I think she can pull the right strings for us." (Since the Pentagon's grand opening for business during World War II, Billie Alexander had been the Airborne and Special Forces assignments lady and had become a living legend.)

I labored through the Special Forces Selection Battery of written knowledge and memory tests for two hours. Figuring that I'd probably busted the thing, a grinning Master Sergeant Harris tossed the graded test sheet down before me. "You scored a 430. Not bad, Walker." I couldn't believe it. I had figured on being reclassified into some safe and secure job, such as virtually repeating basic combat training at Drill Instructor School on Fort Ord. Now here I was yet again on the road to fun and adventure.

My life from that point took on the momentum of a runaway freight train. The first setback Mrs. A made vanish was the P-4 profile. A downgrade to P-3 or lower was required for "probationary" return to parachute status, and with a wave of her magic wand, an amended form appeared in my medical records. To my dismay, I remained excluded from combat duty, a totally unacceptable limitation and one which I'd eventually eliminate. That notwithstanding, I realized that Mrs. A had pulled off a minor miracle, so who was I to complain? Master Sergeant Harris in the meantime had tirelessly cleared the way for me with the Green Beret power elite at Fort Bragg.

The Special Forces Training Group had specified that I be weapons-current prior to reporting in, and a visit to the beach range with Bill Vibbard and Master Sergeant Harris quickly established that I could still accurately—and safely—engage a target with the M-16 rifle and M-60 machine gun. An hour on the post's pistol range brought me back up to speed, and I requalified with the M-1911 service automatic.

The folks were less than elated by the news. In yet another desperate effort to maneuver me into a safer calling, Mom tearfully declared our family having donated more than its share to the country. Dad reprimanded me with an intensity he hadn't shown in years. "You know how Mom feels about your being back in the Army, and now you pull this god-damned crap on her?! If something happens to you, she'll probably die of heartbreak!"

Master Sergeant Harris personally delivered the permanent-change-of-station orders to me. Glancing at the sheet, I excitedly read that I had been assigned to the John F. Kennedy Center for Special Warfare at Fort Bragg. To my infinite relief, I'd be training as a light and heavy weapons specialist.

Gary paled upon seeing the "Sneaky Pete" patch on my shoulder. "What have you gone off and done now? Dad and Mom are gonna have a shit fit when they hear about this." I guiltily told Gary to save his concern as they already knew and left it at that. Leaving the Roadrunner in his care as a bribe, I bade farewell to Fort Ord on February 10.

CHAPTER 9

Special Forces Training

The taxi ride from the Fayetteville airport to Fort Bragg's Smoke Bomb Hill seemed as if I'd been gone a mere day. Checking in with Company D, Special Forces Training Group, Master Sgt. "Rocky" Lane, the holding company senior tactical NCO, stared me down and snarled: "Walker, we don't wear tailored uniforms in Special Forces!" Breaking into a grin, he welcomed me to the training group: "So you're the one-eyed bastard Harris and Mrs. A sent me, huh? See the CQ for room assignment, and we'll be jumping on Normandy tomorrow. Now get the hell out of my office!" I had to admit that these people worked fast.

Trainees were quartered four to a room, and I soon met my roommates—SP4 Tom Weaver, PFC Dave Ensor, and SP4 Bill Holloway. Bill had achieved minor fame in Vietnam during early 1967 through his participation in Operation Junction City and the associated parachute assault of the 173rd Airborne. A *Life* magazine reporter had been aboard Bill's aircraft and taken a photo as he exited. Consequently, Bill's mug made that month's cover. Needless to say, we were all envious of the bronze combat star on his wings. Tom Weaver had served in Vietnam as a Marine rifleman and held the Silver Star, making Dave Ensor the only cherry in our group.

The training group's secretary, Lt. Col. Frank Dallas, had been directly involved in my acceptance for Special Forces training, and he ordered that I be closely monitored during my requalification parachute jump. Like a mother hen, Master Sergeant Rocky rode my tail during our exit from the C-130. I'd logged thirty solo hours in an airplane without bending any metal and managed the landing on Normandy in one piece. Humping together back to the marshalling area, Rocky jovially stated that he supposed I once again rated jump pay.

Life in Delta Company was surprisingly laid-back; even physical training was an unknown. Other than occasional Smoke Bomb Hill work details disbursed from Special Forces' own Slave Market, we hid at the main post cafeteria or in downtown Fayette-Nam's Combat Alley. Conveniently situated between the training group's area and the WAC barracks was the Cannoneers Club, where I'd eventually earn fleeting notoriety.

The three-week Special Forces Basic Enlisted Course, or Phase 1, was Special Forces' answer to boot camp, and it operated at a remote location in Southern Pines known as Camp Mackall. The standard arrival for a class at Mackall was a nighttime combat-equipment jump on Normandy. The weather failed to cooperate, and we were trucked to our new home. Master Sgt. Joe Keating, Phase 1's senior tactical NCO, wasted no time with getting acquainted. Prior to departing post, we had received specific instructions that no non-issue food items or other creature comforts—particularly candy ("pogey bait")— were to accompany us. Keating's painstaking shakedown inspection quickly identified a number of errant individuals, and we were punished en masse with low-crawling through the pea gravel.

A sleepless night in our wooden-frame platoon tents with freezing rain and fifty-mile-per-hour winds whipping the canvas set the trend for our stay. Inevitably, a couple of poorly anchored tents collapsed on the occupants, miraculously causing no injuries. Well before dawn, we were rousted for a grueling two-mile physical-training run led by Staff Sergeant Salinas. I "lucked out," with not only a fifty-pound sandbag in my ruck, but a Browning .30-cal machine gun to haul around. I survived the run—barely—but was rudely awakened to the fact that I was out of shape. Camp Mackall would cure that inadequacy.

Many in the class, especially those relatively new to the military, struggled through the stiff academic curriculum. Since the course material virtually repeated that of my Recondo/LRP training at Fort Campbell, I was spared most surprises. Rather, the real challenges lay in the physical and psychological stresses. We endured sleep deprivation, killer physical training, and minimal chow, all deviously calculated to weed out the unworthy or unmotivated. Ironically, shit-burning detail became a welcome respite since it was the only game available to ward off the freezing cold. Most of us contracted chest colds, and the camp medic shack maintained a bang-up business of dealing out "GI gin," a lethal Army-issue blend of codeine and alcohol. Just guzzle a bottle or two, and Camp Mackall became a warm and fuzzy winter paradise in one's numbed mind.

Successful completion of Phase 1 entitled us to conditional wearing of the green beret, and our Company C platoon tactical NCO, Sergeant First Class Herpers, grudgingly issued them. Proudly pinning the *De Oppresso Liber* ("Liberate the oppressed") crests to our new berets, many of us hummed Staff Sgt. Barry Sadler's "Ballad of the Green Berets." This reward signified only our survival of the basic enlisted course and was in no manner to be confused with full "S" ("flash") qualification.

After a brief recovery period from the Mackall experience, we began domestic and foreign weapons training, known as Phase 2. As with all GIs from World War II onward, our class suffered "M-1 thumb" during initial exposure to the M-1 Garand rifle. Other weapons included, but were not limited to, the Browning automatic rifle (BAR), the M-3 "Grease Gun," and the Russian AK-47 assault rifle. The Russian TT-30 Tokarev pistol, commonly carried by enemy officers in Vietnam, and the German MP-40 submachine gun were especially intriguing.

Special Forces personnel weren't only highly trained combatants, but teachers as well. Every student was required to plan and deliver a block of instruction on a weapon, and mine was the M-1911 service auto. I'd never been much of a public speaker, and despite knowing the subject and my classmates well, the anticipation of stage fright cost me several nights sleep. The moment of truth came, and paralyzed with fear, I pulled up Goose Gosselin's old one-liner of the Russian KP on the submarine. The audience erupted in laughter, and the ice was broken.

I'd been progressing well in training, with a 95 percent academic average, when Sergeant First Class Herpers motioned me aside one morning for a talk. From the first day in Training Group, I had made it crystal clear that I intensely desired to return to Vietnam upon graduation. Herpers almost apologetically stated that in view of my profile limitation, the management preferred my transfer to the 10th SFGA in Bad Tölz, Germany. Following proper protocol, I pleaded my case up the chain of command to Lieutenant Colonel Dallas, who understood and even sympathized with my wish, but he was duty-bound to observe the medical report. It was time to revert to Plan B.

A number of classmates, including Tom Weaver and Dave Ensor, had terminated training mostly due to changes of heart, volunteering for the Vietnam levy. In my case, signing the termination statement in Sergeant First Class Herper's and First Sergeant Snake Olsen's presence was one of the most difficult decisions in my life. Both made sincere, though futile, attempts to retain me in training, but the threat of returning to Europe had me on the run. Now considered just another outcast, I was out of Special Forces and back in the 82nd Airborne before my signature's ink had dried.

I was spared the demeaning ordeal of processing through the Animal Farm. Company B, 2nd Battalion, 325th Infantry (the White Falcons), needed an operations clerk, and I fit the bill. The company commander, Captain Gregg, and First Sergeant Daczyn both seemed to be straight-up guys, and I quickly settled into the job.

The position was extraordinarily boring, and a welcome change of pace soon came with the company's temporary-duty assignment to the U.S. Military Academy at West Point to provide support for their "Plebe Summer" camp. The company moved into a Quonset hut complex at one of West Point's satellite training areas, Camp Natural Bridge, and I resigned myself to the humdrum existence as the escape plan came together.

Just prior to Plebe Summer's end, I typed out a 2496 Personnel Action (formerly 1049) for Vietnam, requesting the 173rd Airborne Brigade. A typical harried officer, Captain Gregg signed it without question, and the blank medical profile form I had obtained from the post surgeon's office at nearby Camp Buckner soon indicated Category 1 "picket fence" medical status. The master plan was underway.

Upon returning to Fort Bragg, a quick visit to the 2nd Brigade's troop dispensary and a link-up with a medic friend enabled my momentary use of the officer-in-charge's signature stamp on the profile form. That chore completed, all that remained to do was hand-carrying the 2496 to division headquarters and sweating out the wait for orders.

Like an eleventh-hour stay from the gallows, the orders arrived at the end of September, specifying the 173rd Airborne. I'd maneuver myself into another LRP assignment with N/75 Ranger at Landing Zone English (Bong Son) upon arrival in-country. Now all I had to survive was the physical and I'd be home free.

During my seventeen-month banishment to civilian life, I'd learned that all brigade and higher-level army reconnaissance units had undergone redesignation. The original LRRP units worldwide had been renamed LRP in late 1967. The LRP designation implied a more aggressive mission from an enemy-elimination standpoint, emphasizing active pursuit and engagement when practical, in addition to straight recon. On January 1969, all army LRP units assumed the lineage and honors of the 5307th Composite Unit (Provisional), better known from its World War II fame as Merrill's Marauders. The new Ranger companies were provided letter designations with V Corps LRP (Europe) receiving Alpha and VII Corps LRP (stateside) getting Bravo, while the thirteen companies in Vietnam received Charlie through Papa (Juliet was not employed because of its feminine association).

Despite my fears of discovery, the physical went off without a hitch. With such a large volume of customers to accommodate, the technician manning the vision-testing machine was in a rush to make happy hour at the NCO club. I sympathized with his predicament and donated $45.00 as I accomplished the left eye test with my right one. We both emerged happy campers.

Once again saying bye-bye to Fort Bragg and Fayette-Nam, I joyously realized that I'd soon be saying hello to Vietnam.

CHAPTER 10

Back in Vietnam

The thirty-day permanent-change-of-station leave was a bummer in most respects. The preceding years with Gary's and my being wounded had taken their toll on the folks' twenty-four-year marriage, and they'd recently filed for divorce. After selling our Wetherbee house, Dad moved to San Francisco and took up house with a topless dancer he'd met in a Broadway Avenue lounge called the Roaring 20s. Meanwhile, Mom had moved into an apartment in Manteca and was dating an Army master sergeant bean counter from Sharpe Depot.

To my discredit, I avoided Mom like the dentist. First, she wouldn't shut off the waterworks when I saw her, and second, I'd been tempted to cancel her new boyfriend Fred's ticket. With twenty-five years in the Army, the guy had never seen combat, but his greatest shortcomings were the hint of an overbearing attitude with Mom and his second-guessing me on returning to Vietnam. Breaking up had been traumatic for both of my folks, and I told the jerk in no uncertain terms that were he to injure Mom emotionally or physically, he'd ultimately have to answer to Gary and me. At least the creep was smart enough not to attempt pulling rank.

Despite her occupation, Dad's mid-forties girlfriend Shelley Roberts was a sweet and giving lady—so much so that she coupled me with her twenty-one-year-old killer-knockout Italian girlfriend and coworker, Cassandra Denio. Our foursome made the rounds of various noteworthy city establishments, such as Big Al's and Funnochio's, and I couldn't buy a drink in most of them. Cassandra and I developed a mutual caring and respect, and she promised to write me overseas. We'd see one another again.

Parting with Dad at SFO was yet another blow to my emotions. In anticipation of boarding time, Dad slyly handed me a packaged wrapped in plain brown paper, instructing me not to open it until I was back in Vietnam. Curiosity overtook me, and I asked him just what in the hell he'd given me. Judging by its size and heft, I'd instantly guessed it to be a handgun. With tears welling, Dad solemnly said, "Wizzo, I picked this up from a retired cop friend in the city, and neither of us could think of any better place for its new home other than as your backup protection." Well, this was typical of Dad, always checking six for his boys.

With my head in a cloud over Dad and Mom's marital demise, I flew to Fort Lewis, Washington. At least Gary was soon due for separation from the service and would again serve as an emotional buffer for the folks, especially Mom.

If Fort Dix had impressed me as being a remnant from the Dark Ages, Fort Lewis set the definitive standard. The World War II–vintage buildings were in total disrepair, and the racial disharmony was plain as day, with the blacks embracing a confrontational style that was returned by the whites. Both sides had their share of drug freaks and miscellaneous other malcontents.

Sgt. Jim Spradlin, an in-country transfer returning to Vietnam from extension leave, was himself destined for the 173rd Airborne, and we linked up for mutual protection from the replacement center's volatile situation. Sgt. John Fowler and Sgt. Jim Butler, both returning to L/75 Ranger (101st Airborne) based at Phu Bai, Camp Eagle, soon completed our foursome. The Devil's Den, a crude representation of a snack bar and beer joint, nondiscriminantly served its Vietnam-bound patrons, and the post MPs earned their pay breaking up the routine racial clashes. Most memorable of these was a near riot resulting from a white's boldly broadcast joke of: "Q: What's true mass confusion? A: Fathers Day in Harlem."

I successfully evaded detection of my medical condition, and on the third day at Lewis, our chartered Airlift International DC-8 departed McChord Air Force Base for Clark Air

Base in the Philippines and Cam Ranh Bay. We'd barely commenced the takeoff roll when Spradlin glumly remarked, "Dave, I hope we haven't just shit in our mess kits by doing this." To the contrary, I felt like a kid on the way to Disneyland. Or maybe Jim knew something I didn't.

We touched down some nineteen hours later at Cam Ranh Bay, where I experienced a sense of vindication and renewed purpose. Soon I'd be back in the action so abruptly stolen from me in 1968—and maybe even take out some gooks in the bargain. As if in defiant reply to this thought, a small group of local Viet Cong commenced pounding the northern end of the runway with 82-millimeter mortars. We had disembarked on the airport's southern end, which kept us out of immediate danger, but the little black geysers and *crunch* detonations were a reality check for everyone. I was actually back in the combat zone and knew I'd pulled one hell of a lulu on the Army.

I had barely set foot in Cam Ranh Bay's 22nd Replacement Detachment when an AG sergeant first class accosted me. "Walker, I have it through reliable sources that you have no business being here. Whatever stunt you pulled back in the world is done, but I'm sending you home on the next plane, in shackles if necessary!" Apparently, a do-gooder captain in the Finance Corps had been aboard our aircraft and overheard Jim and me discussing my wounds.

Leaving nothing to chance, I hadn't surrendered my records packet to the AG REMFs, and Jim truly proved his worth as a buddy. He knew where to catch a C-123 for Phu Cat, which wasn't far from Cha Rang Valley. Well, it truly is a small world, and as we strolled through the Phu Cat terminal, I ran into my Special Forces classmates Tom Weaver and Dave Ensor, who were just returning to C/75 Ranger from in-country R&R. They informed me that an additional couple of our classmates were up at English with N/75 but hadn't yet found out who.

Promising to stay in touch with John, Rick, Tom, and Dave, Jim and I successfully E&E'd to the 173rd Airborne Brigade's rear area at Cha Rang Valley a few hours later in a "borrowed" Air Force jeep. You had to love Jim for his resourcefulness, but

I'd much rather have hopped a chopper ride. While Jim told corny jokes from the driver's seat, I maintained my concentration on the road ahead for landmines and for gooks looking to ambush us from the flanks. The fact that we were unarmed didn't help my psyche. Arriving at Cha Rang in one piece, I remained hyper gun-shy to being exposed, reflexively cringing whenever I saw an MP armband or REMF carrying a clipboard.

In all of the excitement, I'd completely forgotten about the package Dad had given me, which was now buried at the bottom of my aviator's kit bag. I'd also totally disregarded the possibility of a shakedown inspection (which miraculously never took place anyway). With Jim looking on, I unwrapped a mint-condition Walther P-38 9-millimeter pistol with two spare charged magazines and one in the well. Thoughtfully, Dad had also included a twenty-five-round box of ammo. Jim's eyes bulged. With a lump in my throat, I was simply speechless. This priceless gift and I would see many years and miles together.

Cha Rang Valley's main function was to provide newly arrived personnel with basic jungle survival training and facilitate climate adaptation. Jim had been gone only a month, and I'd just left the sweltering North Carolina and New York summers, so we "adapted" at the enlisted men/noncommissioned officers' club.

The one person I'd been waiting for had actually tracked me down. "You must be the Walker I'm looking for. I'm C. J. How would you like to come home with me to N/75 Ranger? We already know about your little problem, so let's dash the hell outta here, and we'll have the orders cut at English. Oh, and somebody you know is waiting for you." Sgt. Chuck Johnson was the headhunter for N/75 and had found me through word of mouth. Try as I might, I couldn't persuade him to give up the source.

I bade Jim a temporary adieu and hopped in C. J.'s jeep for the drive up QL1. C. J. was packing a .45 service auto, and an M-16 rested handily between the front seats. Plus, I had Dad's Walther tucked in my waist as a backup. We passed LZ

Uplift and eventually Bong Son on our way to LZ English, and it dawned on me that my brother Gary had traveled this very road. He had been based at English with the 2nd Battalion, 503rd, and here I was trailing in his footsteps for a change.

Approaching the Ranger-tabbed compound archway on Ranger Hill, I viewed a sign bearing the company scroll, along with the phrase "Live by Chance . . . Love by Choice . . . Kill by Profession." And there, bigger than life, stood Sgt. 1st Class Roger "Hog" Brown. We hadn't seen or spoken to one another since that dark day in Phuoc Vinh in early '68, and it was a joyous reunion. In a real twist, John Fowler was an acquaintance of Roger's and had called him on the sly from Cam Ranh Bay after I'd casually mentioned our knowing each other in F/58 LRP. Roger in turn had ordered C. J. to haul me home. What a great and thoughtful scam! I was finally back home with my own kind!

Ranger Brown immediately kidnapped me into his 2nd Platoon with an assignment to Hotel Team, which was presently on post-mission rest, and following a brief introduction to Sgt. 1st Class (acting 1st Sgt.) Henry Caro, I was directed to the company commander's office. Meeting Capt. R. M. Tanaka (also known as Snakeater 6) was an experience. "Walker, are you a pot or acid-head?" "No, sir!" Captain Tanaka returned a wry smile and dismissed me. "Just so you know, I shoot dopers!" "Not me, sir!"

Warily stepping into Hotel hooch, I met SP4 Chuck Lyons from Kendrick, Idaho, a senior scout observer; Sgt. John Hines, the assistant team leader who hailed from Los Angeles; and senior scout observer Jack "Snowsnake" Ramsland, a Native American from Alice, Texas. All were friendly individuals who seemed inclined to make me feel welcome. I'd soon meet the rest of the team, consisting of senior scout observer/RTO SP4 Dave Blow, team leader Staff Sgt. John Kirk, and Kit Carson scout Hai. My prayers of at least being conditionally accepted by these guys were answered when Chuck Lyons offered me a beer. Jack wasted no time in drilling me on a modification to the lyrics for the tune "All Around the Mulberry Bush": "I don't go out with girls anymore / I live a life of danger / I stay at home and play with myself / Whee! I'm a Ranger!"

Ranger Brown brought me up to speed on how my life was about to change. Regardless of prior experience or training, all new team members were required to attend the two-week company training course conducted by himself, First Sergeant Caro, operations NCO Sgt. 1st Class Jones, and company medic SP5 Mike "Doc" Creamer. I knew the training wouldn't be a problem, but the fact that I was actually back in Vietnam and had nearly zero combat experience finally hit home. Through his conversation with John Fowler, Roger knew that I'd recently completed some Special Forces training but gave me some advice: "The best way to forever alienate these guys is to come across as a know-it-all."

Staff Sgt. John Kirk, the Hotel team leader, had been a steelworker in Pittsburgh, and he immediately broke the ice at our first meeting with his joke of my being blind in one eye and unable to see out of the other. Dave Blow, from Dodge City, Kansas, was a comedian, and our sick senses of humor complemented one another. Our Kit Carson scout, Hai, was a former North Vietnamese Army lieutenant who had rallied to our side under the Chieu Hoi surrender/amnesty program for enemy combatants. Predictably, it would take me awhile to warm up to Hai.

John provided me a brief rundown on the tactical areas of responsibility for N/75. White House wonderboy Robert McNamara's program of "Vietnamization" had been instituted about two years prior, with the intent of South Vietnam gradually assuming the combat role as U.S. troops were withdrawn. In reality, it hadn't worked worth a goddamn. The massive reduction in U.S. troop forces had created a dangerous situation wherein Ranger and other special operations teams were used for baiting large enemy forces, after which a (hopefully) larger U.S. force would finish off the bad guys. Consequently, the company was tasked with gathering intel for not only the brigade's area of operations in Binh Dinh Province, but areas much farther west in Kontum Province to the Laotian border to monitor movement on the Ho Chi Minh Trail, the prime route for enemy infiltration from the north. As a result, many of N/75's missions farther west were conducted under the operational control of the MACV Studies and Observation Group unit at Kontum (also known as Command and Control Central, CCC, SOG Central, or Project Sigma). Many other locales, such as the Crow's Foot, Tiger Mountains, Highland Fish Hook, An Lao Valley, Soui Ca, and Nui Mieus, would soon become my all-too-familiar "playgrounds."

As in F/58 LRP, the 17th Cavalry provided our food. A better alternative was located down the hill at the brigade's "steak house." Gooks ran the place, and the charcoal-broiled "ribeye" steaks (probably water-buffalo meat) were a welcome change. The steak house was also where I'd meet our arch enemies, the 4th Battalion, 503rd Infantry. The "bat boys," as we called them, had us pegged as primadonnas, while we in turn identified them with the black power and white counterculture freaks.

Inevitably, squabbles originating at the steak house between Rangers and line doggies escalated to much higher levels. By self-proclamation, the Rangers had designated a set of ideally situated bench seats (for watching the Vietnamese bands) as verboten to line company personnel. This caused hard feelings with the bat boys, ultimately resulting in "The Night of the Steak House Riot." It began with two Rangers forcibly ejecting two line doggies off our "reserved" benches. One had been stupid enough to wear a white T-shirt with the antiwar phrase "We are the unwilling . . . sent by the undecided . . . to do the unnecessary . . . for the ungrateful" boldly printed in black laundry marker—definitely not in line with the Ranger philosophy. This fueled a punch-out free-for-all that started in the club and eventually worked its way up over a two- hour period to Ranger Hill. Aside from the typical scrapes and contusions, the altercation had generated a number of more serious injuries, like brain concussions and broken bones, inflicted by GI bunk adapters. In the end, everyone lost as the steak house was closed for a week for required repairs.

N/75 had its own little plywood and two-by-four shack for post-mission winding down. We called our club the Ranger Lounge. With its dark and grungy atmosphere, including a slowly rotating ceiling fan, the place could have been the original movie set for *Casablanca*, and I instantly fell in love with it. In keeping with the swankiest five-star stateside nightclubs, an off-duty Ranger could guzzle all of the quarter-priced shots of booze or fifteen-cent cans of beer that he could puke while luxuriating at the twelve-foot-wide plywood bar. It also had the benefit of being a mere twenty-five meters from our hooches, much closer than the quarter mile from the steak house.

A satellite of LZ English, LZ North English (a firebase), was located within sight of Ranger Hill about half a kilometer northwest. One could almost set his watch to the daily H&I fire missions of the deafening 175-millimeter howitzer battery and quad 40-millimeter "Duster" cannons bringing death and destruction upon known and suspected enemy positions in the westward mountain ranges. The 175 took care of the long-distance work in locales such as the Tiger Mountains while the Duster hosed down the closer western foothills and valleys. An armored deuce-and-a-half truck known as the "Widow Maker" was equipped with twin .50-cal M2 machine guns and cruised QL-1 looking for trouble in the various mountain passes. For broader area work, an AC-119 "Stinger" gun ship could be summoned from Phu Cat Air Base for a real light show.

Probably to test my mettle (that is, make me quit the unit), Sergeant Penguinetti from Oscar Team had menacingly shadowed me since day one in the company. "I'd just as soon cancel your ticket as a gook's, Walker!" The guy had served three full tours in-country with LRP-Ranger units and had the thousand-yard stare of a kill-crazy psychopath down to a fine art. I outweighed the guy by a good thirty pounds and figured I could lick him in a fair fight. Fair fights, however, existed only in an earlier life, and I wisely chose to travel the cautious avenue of humoring Penguinetti rather than ending up with a midnight Gerber Mark II blade in my heart. I soon learned from his teammates that this was a standard Penguinetti "newbie" evaluation and initiation ritual, but his oft-repeated threats to kill me as I slept still had me wishing I'd just stayed home. Penguinetti actually turned out to be a nice guy once he'd crossed me off his hit list. There were no free passes in N/75 Ranger.

Two of the special forces students Tom Weaver had mentioned at Phu Cat turned out to be my new Hotel teammates Chuck Lyons and Dave Blow from respective weapons and commo classes immediately preceding mine. A third, Larry Snook on Kilo Team, had been my weapons classmate.

All of my new teammates strove to ease my settling into the company, and I took their constructive suggestions to heart. Since speaking was normally a no-no during a mission, I was relentlessly rehearsed in team hand signals, and John Kirk stressed that I bend every effort in improving upper-body and leg strength ("bush beater muscles") during the training period. The northern Central Highlands triple-canopy jungle that we operated in was unforgiving enough without one's being out of shape. Most significantly, a straggler jeopardized the team. As John K. put it, running bush with a four-to-six-man team could be ten times safer or ten times more hazardous, depending on whether you maintained situational awareness or just blundered through the jungle with your head up and locked.

Sergeant First Class Jones provided an obviously rote introduction to the company training and mission statement: "On behalf of Captain Tanaka, I'd like to welcome you new men to N/75 Ranger. Our mission is to infiltrate small four-to-six-man teams for the purpose of conducting covert operations beyond timely conventional support; conduct long-range reconnaissance operations; develop intelligence; coordinate artillery and air strikes; provide downed aircraft security and aircrew rescue, and finally conduct bomb-damage assessment and POW-recovery operations. Missions of a more unusual nature do, of course, occur from time to time. The training is extremely demanding as is our job, and we expect 110 percent output from all of you. Those of you who don't make the cut will be sent down to a line battalion. And before I forget, 'assassinate' is not uttered in this unit. When a specific human target is identified for elimination, 'terminate' is the operative verb."

The worst problem I encountered over the two-week training course was the grueling PT runs. I had been basically sedentary since Camp Mackall, and it showed through my falling out of the first couple of runs. Between the runs and speed climbing our company rappelling tower in full combat equipment, I was soon physically mission-capable. The second obstacle was an initial hesitance over self-injecting the Atropine antinerve agent syrette (a small squeeze tube hypodermic) during Doc Creamer's first-aid class. From bitter experience in 1968, I wasn't all that partial to having needles stuck in me, but with Doc's encouragement—and Brown's order—I finally jabbed the thing in my thigh.

Two weapons I'd been familiarized with in Special Forces training but never had the opportunity to qualify with were the M-203 (an M-16/M-79 combo in an "over-and-under" configuration) and the one-time-use 66-millimeter M-72 light antitank weapon (LAW) rocket launcher. First Sergeant Caro cautioned that we were to destroy the LAW tube upon use whenever practical. Why? Because the enemy would police up the tube and recycle it as a one-time-use Soviet 60-millimeter mortar round launcher. I'd done well with the M-79 in F/58 LRP, and the M-203 proved no different. We fired training rounds from the LAW for familiarization, and it too was a no-brainer. I'd long beforehand attained proficiency with military explosives such as C-4, TNT, and det cord, but Top Caro refreshed us on their other uses. If a team was on the run and in dire need of an emergency pickup point, Claymores served well to vaporize dense vegetation, while a block of C-4 and a few turns of det cord around inconveniently situated smaller trees cleared a path for string extraction. Lastly—and hopefully never necessary—our explosives would serve to destroy equipment should the team face imminent annihilation ("timber").

It could very well have been that I'd slept through previous classes on personal hygiene and diet for a covert team in the bush, but Ranger Brown provided an attention-getting presentation. Holding a bar of Dial soap in one hand and can of Right Guard in the other, he told us that the gooks could detect a foreign odor, like soap. Our LRP rations had been designed to discourage bowel movements, which the gooks could use to track us by its distinctive American scent. We were also advised to wear our unlaundered bush uniform until it fell of our body.

The training concluded with blessings from Top Caro, and along with several other newbees, I was cut loose for mission participation. I felt ready as could be, and what surprised me was that nobody as yet took issue over my disability. The one demand placed on me personally by Doc Creamer was that I wear nonprescription safety glasses in the bush or when training with weapons or explosives.

Team Hotel was soon assigned a five-day mission in the dreaded Highland Fish Hook, a known VC and NVA stronghold. John Kirk had returned from his aerial visual recon of our box, and during his pre-mission briefing, he cheerfully informed us to expect some fun and games with the NVA. The mission was designated primarily as a prisoner snatch, so in addition to tracking down the little bastards, we'd be tasked to take one or more alive. Just how in the hell we were supposed to do that was beyond my scope of knowledge for the time being.

The day I'd long anticipated arrived, and the fear factor finally surfaced. Here I was again intentionally taking a trip into a no-man's-land populated by people whose sole purpose in life was to kill me. As far as I was concerned, they had taken their best shot at me the last time around, and I had now done enough to ensure that I was the killer rather than the killed.

Per standard operating procedure, new team members were bestowed the privilege of packing the PRC-77 radio and its related goodies, and I was no exception. Dave Blow loved the thing. He also packed a full go-go M-14E2, which he cherished as much as the radio. Just why nobody on the team had thought of it beforehand mystified me, and I couldn't resist the urge to provide Dave's weapon a suitable nickname: The Blow Gun.

Combined with all of the other stuff bogging me down, I found mere walking to be a challenge. The short hike to the "crap table" (helicopter pad) nearly exhausted me despite the cooler temperature of near-dusk, and it was a relief to board the "Starblazers Platoon" of the 61st Assault Helicopter Company Huey insertion bird. A second helicopter platoon within the 61st dubbed "Lucky Star" also provided our air taxi rides.

I watched the pilot's takeoff procedure with interest, and it immediately became obvious that the aircraft was laboring under the extreme weight. I recalled what my flight instructor, R.A. "Dick" Bridgeford, back home in Stockton had told me about helicopters: "They're nothing but a million parts flying in different directions and trying to bust each other!"

Our infil bird was shadowed by two Huey gun ships from the brigade's "Casper Platoon" and by an overhead command-and-control ship for supervision and overwatch. As we progressed ever farther northwest, I gazed breathlessly over the beautiful but hostile environment we'd be residing in for the next few days. Steep karsts covered with immense teakwood trees and deep valleys with meandering streams dominated this end product of some prehistoric volcanic apocalypse. I was almost tempted to tell John that I'd changed my mind and just reverse course back to English. Maybe being a clerk or supervising the garbage truck detail wasn't such a bad fate after all.

I knew it was too late when our pilot executed two bogus insertions followed by the short hop to our actual infil point. The aircraft assumed a ten-foot hover over a pinnacle that appeared to be twenty feet in diameter at most, and we leapt off the skids into near-darkness.

Crash! I landed like a sack of potatoes and had barely recovered from knocking the wind out of my sails when John Kirk motioned me to verify commo and provide a SITREP with our LZ English TOC radio relay team, about fifteen miles away. I whispered: "Snakeater relay, Hotel primary lima zulu secure. Lima papa (listening post) one-five mikes (minutes), then proceed NDP." John gave me a thumbs-up, and still in shock, I feebly returned his grin. After double-checking the radio squelch and low volume settings, I settled into the stressful wait with the guys. The most common time for a team to get hit was immediately after infiltration.

The ominous staccato rumble of the departing choppers' rotor blades echoing off the mountainsides and valley floors quickly waned into an eerie silence and an overriding sense of abandonment. We might just as well have been stranded on the moon. I recall briefly thinking that I'd maneuvered my ass off to get back into this shit, and just maybe I was missing a few marbles as no rational person would have done it.

With Hai assuming point position, the team began a labored descent along a wildlife trail John had spotted during his visual recon. Now I'd taken nature hikes in some pretty rugged terrain—like the John Muir Woods in northern coastal California and Yosemite National Park—but this desolate place seemed more like something out of a National Geographic documentary on Tibet. Why worry about the enemy when one misstep, loss of balance, or loose grip could send you careening down a sheer cliff. Up to this point, I'd managed not to hold the team up, but the painful reality struck that humping this type of terrain was something I'd have to work into by increments.

We reached the NDP about an hour later. Situated on a lower valley hilltop in dense elephant grass with surrounding teakwood and mahogany trees, the team established a wagon-wheel defensive perimeter with command-detonated Claymore mines set out like spokes. As the evening progressed, I was learning what would soon become the familiar sounds of night in the Southeast Asian rain forest. Especially unnerving at first was the taunting cry—*fukkoo! fukkoo!*—of the gecko salamander, lovingly known as the fuck-you lizard. Even the wildlife in this place had a hard-on for GIs! So here I was huddled in a deadly triple-canopy jungle, only to peer up through the dense growth and take in a breathtaking full Asian moon. You could almost reach out and grab it.

At around midnight, we were jolted into high-alert mode with a nearby detonation followed by a ghostly high-pitched human wailing. John H. whispered that a gook had most likely tripped an earlier-planted booby-trap or screwed up while installing one, and that we'd probably run across his left-overs during the mission—a routine occurrence. The wailing soon ceased, and it finally sunk in that we weren't really alone out here.

The team followed the standard operating procedure of two-hour guard shifts. I whispered to my relief, Chuck, that I'd probably be keeping him company with no problem since I was scared like hell. First light came and with it my first cold LRP ration breakfast since Phuoc Vinh in 1968. Jack Ramsland noted my rapid chomping during its consumption and nick-named me "Varmint" on the spot.

Prior to our departing the NDP, John K. pointed out our location on the map and had me KAC the coordinates for practice. I managed not to botch the job, and following a SITREP of the team's continued existence among the living, we departed along a seldom-used trail through the dense rain forest to begin our box recon. At least I'd survived the night without whining or giving our position away, and the team appeared to be satisfied with my noise discipline and situational awareness. Truthfully, I was so hyped up that I imagined a gook or booby-trap behind every bush or bend in the trail, but the wonderful adrenaline rush was back.

At about an hour's movement from the NDP, Hai alerted to the smell of nearby smoke. Proceeding ever-so-slowly, we entered a large rock formation in which we discovered an active cooking fire and fresh sandal tracks. The ground was still moist from a recent rain, and I noted the tracks as being comparatively deep, meaning that the gook who'd made them was packing a fairly heavy load. I quietly informed John of my observation and pointed it out to the team. Hai signaled "enemy nearby," and with my gut flipping and flopping, we fol-lowed the tracks to an area of boulders bordering an immense waterfall and mountain pool.

The roar of the cascading water nixed any thought of detecting the sounds of enemy movement, and we gingerly entered a small clearing within dense hardwood deadfall— an ideal place to be ambushed. As if in a cartoon scene, I spotted the homemade Coke-can Chicom-style "potato masher" grenade sailing in an overhead arc about twenty feet away, its smoking string fuse flailing like a kite's tail.

"Frag in!" I yelled, just as the grenade disintegrated in a bright orange fireball in midair with an ear-splitting bang. With my face now buried in the ground, I felt a minor sting above my outer right eyebrow and a thin warm trickle running down my right cheek. The little suckers had tagged me the first time out. What in the hell was I, a goddamned magnet? The grenade, probably charged with less powerful black powder and other aftermarket junk, had done nothing other than provide us a rude wakeup call. Ramsland yelled for me to get my face out of the jungle floor and do my job, and for a fleeting instant, I questioned my judgment in re-entering active duty, much less returning to this place. Maybe I'd actually have been better off back in the World wearing a Synanon cult toga and tossing rattlesnakes in mailboxes after all. I blindly fired where I thought the thing might have been pitched from.

"Dung lai! (Halt!)," John K. shouted and then fired two semiauto shots at a VC soldier fleeing on the trail paralleling the blue line. Chuck and John Hines meanwhile tossed a couple of frags. Dave Blow studiously guarded our flanks with his Blow Gun while Jack covered our six.

The young VC had taken a flesh wound to his right calf from John K.'s weapon and also had superficial frag wounds. He was obviously scared to death. Planting the muzzle of his M-16 against the enemy soldier's forehead, Hai took the initiative and rudely demanded how many of his buddies had been with him and where were they. Despite Hai's spirited efforts, the VC was too petrified to speak. In a way, I almost shared the poor gook's sentiments as John K. yelled for me to call for extraction with a POW, and we headed for life-preserving high ground. We all knew the guy hadn't been alone, and this was sure as hell a shittier-than-normal place to have a birthday party sprung on us.

Since we'd been compromised, the extraction would take place at a preplanned emergency pickup zone (PZ) about 400 meters away. We'd be lifted and re-inserted at the opposite corner of our box, then backtrack in a zigzag to the contact point. The hope was that maybe we'd flush out whoever had hit us. Of course, *they* would now be expecting somebody to come back on the hunt for *them*. The POW would be flown back to English and handed over to military intelligence.

The move to the new PZ proceeded with no further excitement, and under John K.'s close supervision, I called an artillery fire mission on our recent contact point. The artillery's high-explosive impacts sounded pretty close to me, and I jumped with each detonation. When things had settled down during our LP, John K. took the time to inspect my minor head wound. I'd been struck by a small shard of the aluminum Coke can, and he nonchalantly yanked the thing out with his thumb and index finger. "Well, Dave, now you know that Coke really is the real thing, right?" Here I was hoping for sympathy, and this guy makes light of my wound. Scared shitless but wanting to appear casual, I replied, "Right! And I suppose a 7-Up frag is wet and wild, too, huh?" Dave Blow threw in his two cents: if I lost my right eye, he'd get his precious radio back. Thanks for the concern!

Since time and circumstances permitted, I made it a point to apologize to the entire team for my hesitation when we'd taken the frag. I freely admitted that it had been a reflex survival reaction, no doubt related to safeguarding my good eye. I had also thought for a split second that I'd lost my nerve, but Jack's yelling at me to return fire had snapped me back into reality. The guys must have bought it as they didn't abandon me to survive alone in the jungle. I realized then and there that my worst fear—worse than fear of dying—was being rejected by the team and getting the boot off Ranger Hill, my head bowed in shame as I'm forever labeled a coward—the same fear I'd experienced in the AFEES more than five years before.

The following three days produced no material results, including the probably dead gook we'd heard on day one, and we were uneventfully extracted. During the flight back to English, my thoughts drifted to how quickly everything had happened in my life over the past eleven months. One minute I'd been a misfit civilian living a safe and secure—albeit discontentedly boring—life on the block, and the next here I was again pushing life's envelope in mortal combat. I wondered if anybody else in-country had ever pulled off serving on a LRP/Ranger team with only one eye. I knew it had to be unusual at the very least, and I felt shit-hot.

Following a team debriefing from Captain Tanaka and Ranger Brown, John sent me to Doc Creamer for a better patch job on my "combat" wound. Doc stated that I was entitled to another Purple Heart, and I stopped him dead in his tracks. I didn't want it. Doc agreed to honor my request but said that he could take it only so far—in other words, I shouldn't get myself shot up.

The team's first order of business following debrief was to clean weapons and repack. This served to have us ready not only for the next scheduled mission, but for any action as a reaction force for a team in trouble. I confided to John K. that our recent heavily burdened nature trek had totally wiped me out, and he reassured me that another mission or two would improve my movement technique and stamina. Most importantly, if my performance remained up to standard, he'd sanction my wearing of the company scroll. The scroll was treated virtually as a religious symbol, and to wear it meant one's having been fully accepted into the company and, most importantly, the team.

Christmas 1970 was fast approaching, and I still disbelievingly recognized this to be my second holiday season in Vietnam. In true holiday spirit, the teams prepared gifts. Chuck was a fair artisan and fabricated a cute little tinfoil tree to set atop our Sanyo mini-fridge. The joyous morning arrived with gaily wrapped gifts surrounding the tree and Bing Crosby singing carols on a casette tape. I managed to corrupt Nat King Cole's tune "Merry Christmas" by substituting "dead gooks" for "chestnuts" over the open fire, which drew hearty laughs from Dave and mock indignation from Chuck. Jack initiated the festivities by opening his gift, a Claymore kit. From Dave, I received a new M-67 grenade, still in its cardboard shipping container, and I gave him a new box of non-electric blasting caps and a roll of fresh det cord. The remainder of the team received similar martial presents. After all, it wasn't the gift but the thought that counted. As for Hai, we had passed around the hat and purchased him a Seiko diver watch at our little PX. He was naturally overjoyed as the thing would probably have cost him a year's indigenous-mercenary wages. Overcome with emotion and gratitude, Hai blurted: "Nobuddy ebba gimme suh gip befaw! Yew guys aw numba wun!" I hated to admit it, but the little probable double-agent was growing on me.

Along with a hundred-dollar bill, Dad sent word that Gary, now out of the service, had met and married his next door neighbor, Linda, and that I could anticipate being an uncle around August. Also well received were Mom's Christmas card and her desperate plea for me to write home. I did, giving her the white lie that I was assigned as the company armorer. Cassandra sent one of those glamorous wallet-size photos (who had received the eight-by-ten?). She had dressed alluringly but in good taste, and I wished she'd just worn a Victoria's Secret outfit. As for Dad's cash gift, I hoped it would remain in my wallet longer than the fifty-buck check he'd sent during my last go-around in this place.

The Vietnamese naturally observed customs totally foreign to Americans, and Hai ambushed me one morning by grabbing my hand on the way to chow. There I was in front of God and everybody, walking hand-in-hand with another male, and I didn't know whether to deck the little guy or French-kiss him. John Hines saved the day through his info that male hand-holding in Southeast Asia was a gesture of affection and trust rather than a same-sex pickup maneuver, and I instantly understood that Hai had honored rather than insulted me. Still, I'd have to adjust to this version of male bonding.

Sgt. George Morgan, the Golf Team leader, was fast approaching the end of a six-month tour extension with the company and was due to rotate back to the World. His team had been in the process of extraction from a relatively safe firebase security/radio relay mission in the Tiger Mountains when the safety pin for an M-67 (baseball) grenade secured to his harness accidentally dislodged. The resulting detonation killed George instantly and seriously wounded a young private first class named Jowers, who had been with me at Cha Rang Valley and had less than a month in-country. The kid hadn't lasted as long as I had first time around. As I'd learned earlier, things happened fast in this place, and the only guarantee, assuming one didn't wind up as missing in action, was that he'd be sent home—in one piece, on a stretcher, or in a casket. Morgan's emotional memorial service was the first of four I would attend while serving with N/75.

New Year's Eve fell upon us and brought a trio of Red Cross "donut dollies." For the guys who'd been in-country for a while, seeing an American woman wasn't only a culture shock, but an almost irresistible temptation. Although relatively fresh from the states, I hadn't been serviced lately either, and "Dolly Dimples" would have looked good in a pinch.

The afternoon progressed merrily and harmlessly enough, with the standard Kool-Aid, cookies, and games, but the company had different ideas for the girls. One of the young ladies had been entertaining Hotel Team with news from the World, and we broke out a bottle of our readily available Mateus rotgut wine . . . along with my prosthetic eye. Soon enough, the earlier chaste girl was in stitches over my eye tricks and was harboring more risqué thoughts as we lured her to the Ranger Lounge for the evening's festivities. Her companions in the meantime had undergone similar prepping with the other teams, and with their arrival, a genuine pull-out-all-the-stops party began. Well before the stroke of midnight, we had the ladies attired in camouflage jungle shirts and panties, go-go dancing on the bar top before our lustful audience. Hell, even our company mascots, the puppies Tango and Bullet, were enjoying the show, if their yaps were any indication. Despite the booze and obvious temptation, the ladies weren't violated and all present had a fond memory to cherish.

Getting laid was naturally of no minor concern to us, and the nearby village of Di Duc, located immediately west of LZ English's runway, satisfied us. The place was supposedly run by male civilians nicknamed "cowboys" and was also frequented by enemy personnel. A live-and-let-live truce existed between us, but verbal exchanges were common. "We see you later out in bush, GIs!" "Fuck off, gook!"

It was a given that somebody would sooner or later spoil Di Duc for everyone, and an unidentified trio of N/75 members managed to do so in grand fashion one night. Naturally, they'd packed frags along with the obligatory .45 service autos. A heated argument ensued between our guys and a small group of probable VC soldiers located on the opposite side of a corrugated metal barrier surrounding the ville. The Rangers pitched a couple of frags over the fence in defiance, injuring several of the supposed civilians. Security was thereafter stepped up to the point where an attempted infiltration into Di Duc was virtually impossible, and word went out that anyone caught doing so would be thrown to the MP wolves in Long Binh Jail (LBJ).

To our great distress, just after the New Year, Ranger Brown was seriously wounded with Oscar Team by an AK-47 round to the chest during a mission in the Highland Fish Hook. He was immediately evacuated stateside for treatment, and I wouldn't see or speak to him for thirty years. That he survived to attend Infantry Officer Candidate School and log twenty years of active service is further testaments to his unyielding will and dedication to the Ranger Creed. With this unexpected departure, we inherited Sgt. 1st Class Udo Taring as our platoon sergeant. He and Brown had gone a long way back together as instructors at the Fort Campbell Recondo School and Fort Benning Ranger Committee, and we knew ourselves to be in good hands.

About the same time as Ranger Brown's evacuation, Top Caro was seriously wounded during a rehearsal for a CIA-sponsored heavy team "Bright Light" POW rescue mission in the Dak To area. Located in the northwest corner of Binh Dinh Province on the II Corps/I Corps and Kontum Province borders, Dak To had been the site of one of the Vietnam War's most intense battles, the 173rd Airborne's desperate fight for Hill 875 during Thanksgiving 1967. The place remained a major NVA operational area, as every company team had well learned. The Bright Light mission unfortunately turned out to be a bust since nobody was home (the bad guys had moved the POWs north).

We'd taken a real hit with the loss of two key senior NCOs, and 1st Sgt. Frank Moore came to our rescue from the 4th Battalion. A former Marine and Korean War veteran, Top Moore had joined the Army immediately following Korea and had since become a living legend in Fort Benning's Airborne black-hat community. The guy worked out with two cement-filled five-gallon solvent cans mounted on an engineer stake as dumbbells, for Christ's sake.

The Nui Mieu Mountains were located about thirty klicks southeast of LZ English on the coastline and were an assigned area of responsibility for the company. John K. and John H. had expressed their displeasure over brigade HQ's hare-brained scheme that Team Hotel execute a beach infil as opposed to the usual—and much safer—higher terrain drop-off. Along with the other guys, I knew this insertion scenario to be not only potentially suicidal, but likely the brainchild of some noncombat office crackpot. Who did these people think we were, the Marines? It was as if we'd all read John's mind when he said that our weapons would be rendered useless as soon as the chopper touched down on the beach because the rotor wash would create the mother of mini-sandstorms. We'd be screwed if the LZ were hot, with nowhere to run other than into the South China Sea. Another brigade whiz kid came up with the solution of wrapping our weapons in poncho liners, which would have to be removed before we could return fire. Thanks to both Johns, Taring, and Captain Tanaka, the idea was trashed before anybody got hurt.

Team Hotel ran four uneventful missions in January, during which Dave got back his cherished radio and I inherited another pistol-grip M-79 to accompany my M-16, just as in F/58 LRP. The unmistakable and eerie *whoosh-whoosh-whoosh-thud* of descending shrapnel from friendly night-illumination rounds was often heard, and the nearby impacts were unnerving.

On the fourth mission, we unexpectedly received a two-day extension, and as a result, we learned an important lesson in the rationing of water. The LRP ration, of course, could be consumed dry as a last resort, but the normal practice was to hydrate the thing. Combined with normal maintenance consumption, this caught us by surprise, and we were forced to resort to water obtained from bomb craters. Really delicious stuff, with its orange color, mosquitoes, and deadly bacteria.

Following a mission in the An Lao Valley, John officially okayed my wearing of the company scroll, and I literally wind-sprinted to the tailor shop to get them sewn on my rear-area uniforms. It was as proud a day as when I'd graduated from the 101st Recondo School.

The third (and unproductive) mission in the Soui Ca Valley caught us by our balls. Anticipating an early-morning extraction at a nearby PZ, we'd established a night laager position about ten meters from a dry stream bed, and the fun began shortly afterward. What had been a brilliantly moon- and starlit night suddenly became a torrent of the most intense rain I'd ever imagined, not to mention a nonstop lightning show—my first monsoon downpour. The Claymores went during a lightning strike while the stream became a raging river, transforming our NDP into a two-foot-deep wading pool. Having been totally compromised, all we could pray for was that the gooks weren't crazy enough to be running around in this shit. Extraction time might be another story.

By first light, the storm front had run its course, leaving in its path the usual low cloud ceilings and virtually zero in-flight visibility. Well, our trusty Starblazer rotorheads weren't about to allow such minor technicalities prevent our pickup, and it was agreed that they'd take frequency-modulated radio direction-finder steers off our PRC-77 radio. This enabled the pilot to take a bearing from the aircraft's automatic direction finder pointer needle and fly a homing course to the origin point. Just keep the pointer arrowhead on the aircraft's nose, and you'd get there eventually. The disadvantage was that with repetitive transmissions, the gooks could theoretically triangulate our position. As if we weren't already plagued with enough problems, John K. had discovered an obviously manmade trailmarker pointing in our proposed direction of travel. The only logical conclusion was that Hai had placed it, also raising the disturbing possibility that he'd installed earlier indicators of our movement. Without making his discovery obvious to Hai, John gave us a heads-up. The crystal-clear message was that were Hai to so much as look cross-eyed, he'd become a snack for the wildlife.

Crossing our fingers that the gooks hadn't set up a birthday party for us with Hai's help, we moved out for the PZ. Even the higher ground had become totally saturated from the rains, and moving through the quagmire and dense elephant grass was an exercise in frustration. I was about eight meters in-trail playing follow-the-leader with Hai when my whole world literally fell out from under me. Leave it to the new guy to find a water-filled artillery impact crater! The thing was about seven feet deep, and I remember hitting bottom face-first and dropping my weapon. If the situation hadn't been so potentially dire, it could have been a *Three Stooges* clip. In a panic, I probed the bottom of the crater, finally retrieving the weapon, and on the verge of drowning, I struggled up to where I finally grasped a resurrecting handful of elephant grass. Maintaining a close watch on Hai, John K. greeted my resurfacing with an extended hand.

The PZ was a relatively obstacle-free area about twenty meters wide, but the minor slope and twelve-foot-high elephant grass would require a hovering extraction by the exfil bird. With eyes shifting constantly between our areas of responsibility and Hai, we divided ourselves along the PZ perimeter for security and settled in for the Starblazer's arrival. The weather had remained zero-zero throughout our uphill slog to the PZ, and John K. quietly expressed his doubts about the prospects of the flight crew finding us before they blundered into a granddaddy teakwood tree or mountainside. I agreed with Chuck that the Blazers might not even launch into this shit, giving Hai and whatever other gooks might be around a golden opportunity to ruin our day.

Jack was the first to detect the inbound Starblazer's telltale rhythmic rotor beats. As the bird gingerly probed its path into our location, we all prayed not to be caught below the aircraft. The chopper continued homing in on our signal, and John broke out his strobe light. Out of the mist, as if an angel of mercy wrapped in a halo, first the pulsating blinding beam of the chin landing light, then the bulbous nose of the aircraft with its Starblazer logo, materialized.

I'd gained a rudimentary knowledge of flying during my seventeen months as a quasi-civilian, having logged twenty solo flight hours and probably knew better than the rest of the team that these brass-balled army aviators had pulled off a miracle. The aircraft commander held the bird rock-steady in a three-foot hover as we struggled aboard, and as he pulled pitch out of the PZ into the white void, I think all of Team Hotel said Hail Marys. To our immense relief, John H. disarmed Hai immediately upon the aircraft's achieving stable flight. The ungrateful bastard knew the scam was up, and I think it was all we could do not to just say the hell with it and give the little traitor a free-fall lesson without a parachute. I angrily removed the Seiko watch we'd given him for Christmas.

Other than occasional brief glimpses of the terrain, the initial flight back to English was a real white-knuckler, and I observed the flight crew's actions with great interest. Although the aircraft commander was flying the chopper, the co-pilot had given his undivided attention to navigational information from the aeronautical chart and heading corrections. Since both pilots were on the gauges, the crew chief and door gunners served as lookouts for the "minor" issue of terrain avoidance. All we could contribute were terrified expressions.

We broke out of the soup about fifteen miles northwest of English, and with sighs of relief, we were soon back on terra firma. The chopper crew had gone the extra mile while bailing us out, and every drop of free booze we poured down their throats later that evening at the Ranger Lounge was a premium payment on life insurance from our viewpoint.

As for Hai, Captain Tanaka had him out of the company and in the custody of military intelligence as soon as we'd touched down on the crap table. The incident created quite a stir concerning the remaining indigenous company scouts, and all were thoroughly interrogated as potential collaborators with Hai. John K. also made it abundantly clear to all of us that although he hadn't out rightly brought up the subject beforehand, we'd be judge, jury, and executioner in any future similar situation.

Hired enemy expatriates weren't the only source of compromising company operations and individual teams. Indigenous females from the nearby villages of Di Duc and Sai Wen, known as "hooch-maids," were commonly employed in the company area for cleanup chores, laundry, and other jobs. Was it just coincidence that the gooks often seemed to be present with a greeting party during or shortly after an insertion, or were the mama-san hooch-maids providing them with advanced notice? All it took was carelessness on one's part—an unsecured map overlay, an eavesdropped briefing . . . the possibilities were endless. Of common knowledge to everyone was that immediately prior to a major mortar and rocket attack on LZ English during 1968, a number of civilian employees had been observed to have apparently been pacing off key areas, such as Ranger Hill. Ironically, you could leave an expensive watch lying on your bunk, depart on a mission, and find it there upon your return. It had repeatedly been drilled into us from day one in-country that no indigenous civilian could be totally trusted.

A cardinal sin in any combat unit, but especially with small covert teams, was getting separated from the main body. We'd been moving through the Highland Fish Hook just before nightfall when the team halted for a break. I'd been pulling rear security, was bored to tears, and managed to fall asleep in a matter of seconds. Most people have experienced the sensation of dozing off only to snap awake in a panic, which is exactly what I experienced. For a few terrifying seconds in the darkness, I thought I'd been left behind. I immediately moved in our direction of travel about five meters, only to hear Dave Blow's whispering inquiry of what in the hell was I doing. Never again did I catch unplanned sleep on a mission.

Nearby LZ North English had among its residents a company of Republic of Korea Army (ROK) personnel. While visiting with a buddy assigned to the quad-40 duster unit one morning, I discovered that whatever martial discipline I'd experienced in our army paled in comparison to that meted out by the ROK officers and noncommissioned officers. While observing an in-ranks inspection, I witnessed an ROK NCO strike an obviously errant individual of lower rank full force in the face. The poor soul went down, and the NCO delivered a roundhouse tae-kwan-do kick to the man's head. Unbelievably, the victim jumped to his feet in a ramrod-straight position of attention.

This barbaric treatment by ROK seniors of their own troops also carried over to POWs. A story circulating in our company area had it that an ROK officer at North English had been harshly interrogating two NVA POWs to no avail. The officer finally had enough silence from the first subject, drew his sidearm, and blew the gook's brains out. The gook's sidekick thereafter spilled his guts like Hoover Dam breaching. The official policy in N/75 was to treat POWs humanely. The unofficial policy was to employ whatever means necessary to extract information if the team were to find itself in dire straits.

Getting done in by the gooks or our own guys wasn't necessarily the only way to get killed in Vietnam, even in the relative security of the company area. An excellent example was the normally mundane task of burning company trash. Team Hotel had been delegated to do so in our lower company perimeter burn pit, and we filled the thing to capacity with LRP-ration and sundry-pack boxes, empty grenade canisters, and ammo crates—the usual junk. Normal practice was to pour a small amount of diesel or gasoline in the pit and ignite the pile with a lit scrap of cardboard. Well, leave it to Dave Walker to come up with the brilliant idea of initiating the thing with a hand-launched parachute flare. I took aim at center of mass and smacked the firing-pin cap with my palm. What we got was an out-of-control rocket that initially ricocheted off the pit wall, then took free flight toward me. I felt the rocket plume's intense heat as it missed my head by mere inches, ultimately striking the hillside in a dying series of wild loops and gyrations.

The company routinely had visitors attired in civilian sport clothes with crew cuts and aviator sunglasses. The gifts they bore, such as remote-control devices for electrical widowmaker ambushes and silenced Beretta 9-millimeter pistols, were proof-positive that these guys weren't USO reps. Unlike our Ranger Lounge chopper pilot guests, a few of the spooks seemed never to have heard of buying a drink, despite our generosity.

A minor restructuring of team assignments was necessitated with Hai's departure and the wounding of the Mike Team leader, Gary Bushinger. Gary's Kit Carson scout Sam (also known as Nam Si Do) had also been hit. John Hines went to Mike as their temporary team leader while we picked up Sgt. Kent Farrand as our assistant team leader. Kent, an earlier Team Hotel member from Oklahoma City, had been working the TOC because of his relatively brief time remaining in-country and volunteered to return to the bush without a second thought.

With Hai down the road, SP4 Ronald K. Wooley, from the bayous of Lake Arthur, Lousiana, became our newest member.

Ron had been turning wrenches down the hill with the brigade's Company D maintenance unit and had expressed a desire to pursue a more interesting life. Tall and lanky with a pronounced Cajun twang, Ron had ears like Dumbo the elephant. I immediately expressed my belief to Ron and the team that he'd been raised in a very rural environment, taken to the extremes of residing in a house perched on stilts to minimize alligator and snake visitors, and had been receiving compulsory small-boat training prior to beginning preschool. In view of the latter, I could think of no more appropriate a nickname for Ron than "Swamp Rat." Chuck meanwhile drew cute little alligator caricatures of the mayor of Lake Arthur, "Al E. Gator," and his faithful aide-de-camp, "Croc O. Dial," to pin on our hooch wall. Swamp Rat seemed to meld well with the team, and we'd be short a man for only his training period.

I met an SP4 named Josh from the D Company maintenance unit at the steak house, and he'd managed to drastically modify a Colt XM-177 Commando (CAR-15) into a spitting image of a Flash Gordon ray gun—through generous use of cotter pins, cutting, brazing, and in general totally bastardizing the thing. He sold it to me for the measly sum of $75. Proudly showing the thing off to our guys the next morning, John K. strolled into the hooch. Confident that I'd made Josh the sucker of the century with this opportune deal, I showed John my acquisition. He stared blankly at my new pride and joy, then told me that I wasn't taking it anywhere, that it would only jam or blow up in my face. I took a forty-buck loss when I sold it to an SP5 Casper crew chief who also thought it looked macho. His pilot most likely threw a fit similar to John's.

Staff Sgt. Walter Solgalow, better known as "The Mad Russian," was the Oscar Team leader in the company and the only person to make issue of my one-eyed status. Initially, I let his snide references to me as "the one-eyed freak" roll off my shoulders, but during a company barbecue one day, I decided that enough was enough. As usual during such events, Team Hotel had been guzzling our Mateus wine, and I was thus well primed for a confrontation with the Russian. Catching him near our TOC with ample onlookers, I drunkenly told him that I was going to whip his ass for poking fun at me. At about the same time that I launched a sluggishly executed right cross, the Russian clipped me right in the face. Top Moore yanked me up by my shirt collar like a misbehaving schoolboy and dragged me back to Hotel hooch to sleep it off. I learned the next morning that the Russian, a Ukrainian native, had been a semi-pro boxer in civilian life and that he'd generously pulled his punch—at least all of my teeth had remained in place. I swallowed my pride and apologized to Walter, and he never put me down again through word or action. Top was a different ballgame: "Walker, don't you *ever* swing on one of my senior NCOs again or I'll hang your half-blind ass out to dry on the company archway!" "Yes, Top!"

John's prediction of my adapting well in the bush had become reality. He further stated that I seemed to have a natural aptitude for operating in the jungle, including tracking and detecting booby-traps. Consequently, my new job on the team (which I very much wanted) would be alternating point/slack with Chuck. I wasn't the king of the hill in this respect, however, as SP4 Bobby Cantu of Kilo Team possessed 20/10 vision (to my 20/15) and could probably detect fire ants screwing at night.

Once again at full strength with Swamp Rat's successful completion of training, Team Hotel was assigned an unusual—and for me embarrassing—mission in the Crow's Foot area during early February. Yet another "fast burner" at brigade had come up with having a scout-dog team accompany us. Don't get me wrong, the scout-dog concept worked well with large units in less demanding terrain, but like almost everywhere the company operated, the Crow's Foot consisted of steep mountains and triple-canopy rain forest. We weren't in the business of providing dog handlers on-the-job LRP instruction. Besides, the terrain and general environment would take its toll on the dog. We'd also wind up having to pack the dog's food and water and maintain a watch on the handler to ensure he didn't blunder us into some inescapable nightmare.

Established in our NDP during the first night, the dog silently alerted us to movement about ten meters to my direct front. We had a full moon, and as what I thought to be a gook approached ever closer to our position, I prepared a grenade for deployment. I was finally able to detect the disturbance of brush by a discernible humanoid figure when from out of nowhere I was suddenly getting beaten on like a bastard child. It was an orangutan, and as fast as he'd whooped my ass, he'd dashed back off into the jungle. With my shaking continuing for a time afterward, the rest of the guys were unable to contain stifled laughs. Hell, the dog even stared me down.

It became evident early in the mission that the dog, a beautiful pure-bred German shepherd named Chino, was having a rough go of it. Contrary to what we'd anticipated, the SP4 handler proved to be a minimal burden and surprisingly bush-savvy. Still, he was totally focused on taking care of the dog rather than searching for gooks, and with no injured feelings or anybody hurt, we chalked it up to yet another experience in Vietnam. Like the proposed hare-brained Nui Mieus "beach assault," the idea was dropped like a hot potato. The dog team had shown a lot of guts, however, and we treated Chino to raw steak with Tango and Bullet while we got the handler smashed in the Ranger Lounge at mission's end. As an ultimate gesture of goodwill, we awarded the team two company scrolls, one for Chino's collar and one for the handler as honorary keepsakes.

The middle of February produced a truly off-the-wall mission for Team Hotel. Some top-secret spook outfit had appropriated N/75 to act as tour guides for a two-man seismic-sensor installation team in an area of operations well west of Dak To. They'd be planting the things on Ho Chi Minh Trail branch-offs, and John joked that he'd heard the gizmos couldn't discern a seventy-five-pound Vietnamese from a bull elephant. Yet another ineffective and dangerous waste of valuable manpower. The guys showed up armed with .45 service autos. Admittedly, the long tubular devices they had to pack made it awkward for them while packing a rifle. Although friendly enough, their spanking-new uniforms and boots were dead giveaways to their full-time REMF status. As the mission progressed, the constant wheezing, stumbling, and falling made it obvious that neither technician had ever been in the bush, and the two-day ordeal couldn't have ended soon enough for us. They weren't bad guys—they just didn't belong in no-man's-land placing a team at risk. We just had to wonder what kind of bozo with his head in the ionosphere came up with this kind of resource-devouring science-fiction shit.

Every mission had its unknowns, and an early-February insertion in the Highland Fish Hook bore this out for Team Hotel. We'd been observing our standard cautious movement through the triple-canopy rain forest when I observed a relatively clear area and what appeared to be scorched sheet metal off to our right front. Halting the team in its tracks and listening for any sign of movement, I signaled John K. to my point position for a better look and a second opinion. Continuing our snail's pace toward the object, we discovered it to be a downed UH-1 Huey helicopter. A cautious inspection of the wreckage produced grisly results. The aircraft had obviously experienced in-flight problems or been shot down and had been nearly consumed by fire upon impact. Contained within and immediately surrounding the wreckage were the blackened skeletal remains of the crew, but all weapons and surviving ammo had been removed, obviously by the gooks. John noted that remnants of the flight crew's helmets were of the early-war issue white, implying that the wreck had been there for years. John was able to decipher a portion of the aircraft registration number, which was promptly submitted to the appropriate headquarters at mission end. A closer search for dog tags proved fruitless as they'd either melted in the fire or had been snatched up by the gooks. We never received word of the date of loss or identities of these heroic men who had sacrificed their lives in direct support of folks like the now very humbled Team Hotel.

Chuck and I were supposed to be shit-hot point men, but two incidents during a mission in the Highland Fish Hook proved that perfection occasionally falters. We'd made light contact just before nightfall and had broken away through no choice on a high-speed trail. Because of darkness and the severity of the terrain, TOC had decided that an extraction was impractical until first light. I was on point, and having never done so during darkness, I was taking my time. I figured our time on earth had come to an end when I heard a light rustle followed by snoring. What a pro! I'd just blundered the team into an NVA bunker complex of unknown size. Through a miracle, not an enemy soul was awake, and we backed out like caterpillars on downers.

We departed our marginal NDP well before first light, upwardbound for the PZ with Chuck now on point and me as slack. About halfway up, we heard a barely perceptible pop. Chuck looked back at me in wonderment with a shrug of his shoulders, and it was then that I spotted the broken tripwire. Chuck traced it from the secured end to the point of separation, where there was a dud 750-pound GP bomb. The gooks had rigged a moisture-contaminated smoke-grenade fuse to a wad of some stale homemade explosive, which was then placed over the bomb's fuse. Had the contraption functioned as intended, there wouldn't have been enough of us left to scrape up with an X-Acto knife.

Continuing upward, we detected first the distant sound of breaking brush, then unchecked voices. It didn't take a rocket scientist to figure out that the residents of our prior night's bunker complex had picked up our trail. John K. immediately deduced that our tits would soon be in a wringer, and Blow instinctively got on the radio to give the extraction and support birds a little incentive for running full throttle.

Still in near-darkness and with the gooks in pursuit, we finally reached the PZ, which turned out to be totally unacceptable for a landing or even low-hover extraction. Considering the fifty- and sixty-foot-high trees cluttering the PZ, a McGuire extraction would be required. Blow advised the birds of our predicament. Because of the low visibility, we'd have to activate a magnesium trip flare and strobe light to mark our position. Meanwhile, John called in a standby artillery mission on the bunker complex we'd discovered. The idea was that once we were safely out of range, the arty folks could hammer the shit out of the place with an airborne forward observer.

Our pursuers hadn't lost any enthusiasm, and John ordered that when the extraction bird was on short final, we'd be conducting a "mad minute" with weapons and frags as a delaying action. As an added precaution, the last man to snap in would give the area a final hosing down with a magazine and frag.

Despite the darkness, our extraction chopper found us with no hassles, and we progressively snapped into the line. My weapon had a field-expedient 550 cord suspension line rifle sling attached, and I'd stupidly looped it around my neck just prior to hooking up. As I was being yanked up through the trees, the thing became entangled on a small branch and damned near choked me to death before the thin branch broke, not to mention nearly causing the loss of my weapon. Like the rest of us, I was scratched and beat to shit during the ascent. Jack's last-second hammering of the area with his M-203, combined with the chopper door gunner plastering downhill with his M-60, kept the gooks at bay, and we made it out, relatively no worse for wear. With sufficient light now available to the chopper crew, we were gently set down on a fairly safe and open area about two klicks from the extraction point, where we were permitted to board the aircraft.

Safely back in the rear, we learned that an NVA reinforced rifle company had been attempting to sandwich us in for the kill. My legs might have been like rubber, but I was on an adrenaline high like I'd never experienced. This stuff just got better with the increased risk!

Sound asleep in Hotel hooch the next morning, we were rudely awakened by loud and penetrating detonations.

Rushing out the back door for a look, we observed a spectacle that few live to tell about. Far to the southeast, in the vicinity of LZ Uplift (about fifteen klicks away), were immense clouds of black smoke, the product of a U.S. Air Force B-52 Stratofortress "Arc Light" strike on heavily fortified enemy positions. Even from our relatively distant vantage point, the fireballs and shockwaves were awe-inspiring and the concussions unbelievable. Despite the distance, we could feel the changes in atmospheric pressure caused by the rolling shockwaves, which even produced minor nausea in us.

Considering Team Hotel's most recent mission, Captain Tanaka decided that each team should pack an M-60 machine gun with bipod removed, and with Ron Wooley's recent completion of company training, we now had a soldier who would prove to be a born gunner. Dave Blow immediately expressed his total lack of desire to hump the thing ("I'll never divorce my Blow Gun!"), and Swamp Rat put his best foot forward through volunteering. The gunner would pack 500 rounds of machine-gun ammo while the other members, excluding the RTO, would each haul 100—not a huge price to pay for the gun's potential to pull us out of a terminal bind. Dave would meanwhile continue providing Swamp Rat on-the-job training on the radio.

A mission in the Tiger Mountains proved fruitful for Swamp Rat's standing on the team, not to mention getting his cherry busted. Since day two, we'd detected signs of fresh movement by a probable large NVA force. It wasn't just the Commie sneaker tracks or freshly broken vegetation—we could actually feel and smell these guys. The most fun part was that they probably knew we were shadowing them.

The shit hit the fan on day four as we were preparing to depart our NDP in dense rain forest to parallel a well-used trail. Jack was on his usual tail-end-Charlie position, with Wooley as his slack, when we heard Jack launch a 40-millimeter high explosve to our rear, instantly killing an NVA point man. Swamp simultaneously hosed down the same area with his beloved "Pig," literally cutting the gook slack man in two. Meanwhile, I'd spotted two gooks about twenty-five meters to our right front on the high speed we'd been paralleling. I dropped one in his tracks while Chuck took care of the other. Dave immediately called in a contact report to English, and with position data provided by John, he arranged to have us yanked at a nearby mountaintop.

Realizing that the gooks were most likely attempting to trap us in a horseshoe-style ambush, we became engaged in a running fight, stopping for a brief LP every 200 meters or so. Well, the gooks had no intention of allowing a LRP team to escape, and with the constant breakaway actions, our available ammo soon became an issue. John figured that we were being chased by a probable heavy point element for a company, and their commander's smart tactic was to run us dry on ammo, then finish us off. John advised that were things to go totally down the shitter, we'd set up a tight wagon-wheel defensive perimeter and blow our claymores as the gooks overran us. Although it offered small consolation, at least we'd take a few of them with us. With my stomach turning somersaults, I recalled the first verse of our company motto: "Live by chance." I sure as hell hoped we weren't about to become the subjects of a body-recovery mission.

When we'd reached a (hopefully) safe distance from the initial contact point, John called in 105-millimeter artillery support in hopes of at least impeding the gooks' pursuit. Even with the dense stuff we were in, the 105 impacts were teeth jarring and deafening. Worse yet, John instantly figured out that they were way too close and began making frantic "Check fire!" calls with the Redleg FDC. John was normally one of the coolest people I'd observed, but the developing situation had even him in hypersurvival mode. As for the rest of us, how could we describe being too scared to know we were scared? Amidst all of this excitement and raw fear, however, Wooley unbelievably grinned and stuck his tongue out like a kid teasing his playmates.

The gooks had obviously stayed dead on our heels, and John made the risky decision to take the high speed to the base of our extraction point, then jag up the mountainside.

This would hopefully at least give us the high ground until the cavalry arrived. John had kept the artillery walking behind us, but it hadn't seemed to produce the desired effect. We could hear the gooks conversing in normal tones a couple of hundred meters away. It was clear they were preparing for the coup de grace.

We'd made it to about 150 meters from the extraction point when all hell broke loose from downhill. Kent Farrand was the first to detect movement to our left and right and downward in what was obviously a fan assault formation. Then the gooks employed the old sucker's trick of probing fire to attempt to flush out our exact position. Meanwhile, John was on the radio advising our Casper gun ships that they'd better pour on the coal or we'd shortly be history.

I had decided to conserve my M-16 ammo and yanked the M-79 off my ruck. Jack watched uphill while we placed Wooley at our downhill center with the M-60. Kent had just tapped Chuck and me on the shoulders, whispering that the gooks would probably begin their assault shortly when the heavenly sound of choppers materialized in the distance. As if on cue, the gooks started really pouring it on us—or so it seemed with the surrounding vegetation disintegrating from bullet impacts. We were literally pinned down, and from out of the din came a loud *whoosh-bang-bang*. With eyes as big as saucers, John yelled that we were being probed by RP-7 rockets and that sooner or later the little creep launching them would get lucky.

Casper arrived on station, having taken sporadic fire from our downhill direction, and instructed John to pop a smoke. The plan was for the Casper guys to fire up the entire area of our flanks and downhill, then have us make a run for the extraction point. This was all well and good except for the fact that the gooks had a nasty habit of monitoring our radio frequencies. Therefore, it was vital that the team and the gun ships be on the same page with the color of smoke since the gooks most likely had their own supply. More than one aircraft had been blown out of the sky when homing in on gooks posing as the good guys. As if we hadn't already figured it out,

Kent yelled for everybody to hug dirt as the gun ships started doing their work. Between their M-60s and 2.75-inch rockets, we all felt as if we were inside a blender. Over the incredible racket, John screamed for us to get out of there, and we began a frantic scramble up the mountainside. It felt like a dream, with the bogeyman in pursuit and me weak-legged, constantly stumbling, and unable to prevent being overtaken. Casper meanwhile maintained covering fire while Jack and Wooley mowed down two of our pursuers.

As we reached the mountaintop, the Starblazer extraction chopper was about a quarter of a mile out, with the door gunners having a mad minute on suspected gook positions. As the bird began its low hover on the PZ, the crew chief motioned frantically for us to get the hell on—as if we needed further incentive! Pulling pitch out of the PZ, the door gunners were hosing down the area for all they were worth. All of us meanwhile were skip-breathing from the adrenaline rush. Out of sheer spite and joy, I blindly popped a couple of M-79 high-explosive rounds, which probably managed to kill a few tree branches.

The gun ships remained on station for a time following our departure, keeping the gooks' heads down while waiting for the artillery to resume. The artillery would saturate the area until a reaction line company from English arrived to clean up the gooks and conduct a bomb-damage assessment.

My knees nearly buckled as my boot soles contacted the crap table. My teammates reassured me that I wasn't the only one of us with a pucker factor the size of a Daisy BB. Later in the day, we learned that we'd been playing chicken with a fresh NVA reinforced rifle company infiltrating from a Ho Chi Minh Trail branch. Because of the work performed by the gun ships, artillery, and line reaction company, more than 100 enemy had been killed, along with the numerous weapons and ordnance that were discovered. Team Hotel had also made its small contribution.

A mission in the Nui Mieus during early March proved especially rewarding for Team Hotel. The mission had been designated as a POW snatch, and we hadn't discovered signs of recent enemy activity until the fifth day, March 12, 1971. Setting up an LP in a rock formation with the intent of chowing down, John installed two command-detonated Claymores at offset angles to our front. The intent was merely to wound the first two or three members of an approaching enemy force. John was the first to hear nearby movement in our direction of travel, and as we stared down the trail, voices and the unmistakable movement of brush confirmed that we had human company. Dave called in an imminent contact SITREP as John smiled and whispered: "We're gonna ruin their day!"

Now alerted, we assumed firing positions around the boulders, and at first sight of the enemy point man, John blew the Claymores. I'd apparently taken insufficient cover from the Claymore's back blast and immediately felt an intense stinging sensation in my left inner elbow. No time to fret about that: we were having a mad minute on the gooks. We'd totally surprised these guys and hadn't received return fire, but the question still remained as to how many we had engaged. For safety's sake, the entire team maintained a good base of fire for about a minute, with liberal volleys of M-79 and pitched grenades for good measure.

John was bleeding like a stuck pig from a wound below his right eye and frantically asking Kent if it looked serious. He'd detonated the Claymore from a totally exposed position and caught a respectable chunk of the case in the back blast. I recall hoping that he hadn't just made himself a member of my club. Like a dummy, I'd also managed to catch a small Claymore chunk in my left elbow.

John appointed me to check the kill zone, and prior to leaving cover, I pitched several frags. Moving around the left side of our large boulder, I tripped over a dead NVA soldier who had been literally shot to shit by Swamp Rat. Now I had his blood and guts all over my sleeves and chest, and the additional stench of the guy's evacuating bowels had me on the verge of gagging.

Moving into the kill zone with the rest of the guys providing sufficient cover, I encountered another KIA. The stock of his AK-47 had been shot to pieces, and he'd taken numerous slugs and Claymore goodies. I removed and placed his weapon and web gear at a safe distance should he resurrect himself from the dead and moved on to another lifeless enemy on the trail. This soldier lay on his stomach, apparently dead, and as I warily rolled him onto his back, he opened his eyes in stark terror. I hadn't bargained for this, and for that split second, the young NVA soldier and I shared a bond possible only in war. I literally held the power of God in my hands to take his life and instead asked him a one-word question: "Nook? (Water?)" He weakly smiled and nodded yes as I gently raised his head and gave him a drink from my canteen. Problem was that he'd taken a Claymore pellet in his throat, which had partially damaged his airway and esophagus. The poor little soldier's gagging told me that he'd do much better without my attempting to drown him. I remember thinking how ironic it was that only mere seconds earlier, I'd been trying to kill this guy, who was probably my age, and now here I was in a touchy-feely situation with him. The emotions and instincts in this place routinely ran the gamut of every which way but normal, and a civilian wouldn't have understood it.

Acknowledging my thumbs-up of all being clear in the kill zone, Jack and Swamp joined me to police up the weapons and gear along with the young POW while I moved farther up the trail for possible additional enemy casualties. Other than blood trails, the rest had escaped our wrath.

The company had immediately dispatched Oscar Team as a reaction force upon Dave's call, and prior to evacuating the captured equipment and POW, I removed the POW's pistol belt, complete with NVA NCO buckle, as a war trophy. He was completely limp with shock and fear and had to be carried to the uphill LZ. Team Hotel was extracted while Oscar remained in the area to hunt down our escapees and develop the situation.

Arriving back at English, we provided a debrief to Captain Tanaka and Sergeant First Class Jones. Meanwhile, John was sent down to B Med. and then the 65th Evacuation Hospital in Qui Nhon for care of his eye wound. The piece of Claymore junk that I'd received in my left elbow hurt like hell, and Doc Creamer once again came to the rescue with a removal and patch job. The three-eighth-of-an-inch-wide gray-green case fragment had embedded itself about a quarter of an inch in my elbow, and Doc stated that if the thing festered up, he'd have no choice but to send me down to B Med. for thorough irrigation, packing, and suturing. Like the stubborn dummy I was, I told Doc to just put iodine and a bandage on the thing and give me a bottle of tetracycline.

Sergeant First Class Taring entered our hooch with an order to hurry with our repacking and cleaning up. Very much pleased by our afternoon's accomplishments, Captain Tanaka had decided to place Team Hotel on a three-day in-country vacation to Da Nang's world-renowned China Beach R&R center. He would soon regret this well-meant gesture.

Soon settled in a deuce-and-a-half's bed for the ride to Phu Cat Air Base, Kent begged and pleaded that I souvenir him the pistol belt I'd appropriated from the POW. Kent was really a stand-up guy in my eyes, and I relented to his request.

Dropped off at Phu Cat's security gate, the problems began immediately. An air policeman manning the shack had taken note of our weapons and web gear, complete with magazines and frags, and politely requested that we secure them in a nearby Conex container. What initially pissed me off was the airman's camouflage uniform and spit-shined jungle boots. Sufficiently fueled by postmission anxiety and the Mateus wine we'd all consumed during the trip from English, I smacked the policeman and relieved him of his sidearm. When we'd advanced about fifty feet from the gate, I kicked the .38 service revolver across the tarmac back to him.

The situation really deteriorated upon our entry into the base's NCO club. The Air Force master sergeant master-at-arms had zeroed in on our being armed and made a heroic effort to control our behavior. "Guys, please let us secure your weapons and ordnance, and we'll all be happy campers." By this time, Team Hotel was on a roll, and we weren't about to listen to any mealy-mouthed crap from the U.S. Air Force. After we had ordered six screwdrivers apiece, Wooley was soon feeling his oats through guzzling the drinks followed by smashing the glass and chewing the shards. This exceeded even most of our plateaus of misbehavior, and an immediate proposal was made that we implore John to award Swamp the company scroll immediately upon his return from the hospital.

At our arrival, the club had been filled to capacity with Air Force personnel, but the normal clientele, adequately—and joyously to us—spooked by our behavior, had soon dwindled to only our five-man group in the barroom's center. Well stoked and with no one left to intimidate, we finally relented to the master-at-arm's desperate peace offering of an air-conditioned Quonset hut to flop in and a promised wakeup call for our early-morning flight to Da Nang.

Nursing crippling hangovers the next morning, we were bussed to Phu Cat's ATCO terminal for the trip north. The short flight to Da Nang Air Base in the C-123 Provider was nauseating. Not having eaten for two days, we had nothing in our stomachs to upchuck, but the dry heaves we endured were probably worse.

The wary expressions on the Air Force personnel during the short hike from the Da Nang ATCO terminal to the Army liaison office were proof enough that our previous night's activities had followed us. Naturally, we did nothing to discourage their fears, and Jack's loud query about where to find the NCO club probably put the entire place on red alert. With exaggerated courtesy, the liaison NCO, obviously in a hurry to be rid of us, motioned us out the door to our bus. Still buzzed from the previous evening's partying, I boisterously stated that

Team Hotel was just getting started with its REMF N/75 Ranger awareness program.

The China Beach R&R center was one of two hastily constructed "tropical paradises" in Vietnam. The other, Vung Tau Beach, was located south in the III Corps TZ and far removed from active combat. With Da Nang on the other hand, all one had to do was head a few klicks west to wind up in no-man's-land.

Unlike Phu Cat, the China Beach honchos weren't about to put up with Team Hotel wandering drunkenly about with dangerous articles. An Army R&R center representative wearing a Special Forces combat patch and Combat Infantryman Badge diplomatically stated that he'd secure our weapons and return them upon our departure. Kent figured Team Hotel had already exceeded the envelope's limits, and we yielded to the sergeant's request.

The Army had made a sincere effort to provide comparative creature comforts in the center: stateside-issue bunks with real mattresses and sheets, hot and cold running showers, a movie theater with a snack bar and ice cream parlor, and an open-air bar on the beach. After we'd had our quota of body surfing for the afternoon and stuffed some real stateside-style burgers in our guts, we transferred operations to the bar's large patio. A sweet young Vietnamese girl named Mai catered to our every whim, and we were soon creating new hangovers. Jack occasionally marched to his own drummer and took off for points unknown, probably in search of getting laid.

The previous night and the afternoon had taken a toll on our bodies, and we retired to the barracks for some much-needed shuteye. Our peaceful slumber was abruptly interrupted at around midnight with what sounded like nearby gunshots. Instantly reverting to alert mode, we ran outside and observed red star cluster pen distress flares being launched in horizontal flight paths. A loud megaphone voice barked, "Drop it!" and a brief unintelligible argument ensued. Woozily realizing that we weren't under attack, we went back to the racks.

We arose for morning chow, and Kent was the first to notice Jack's vacant and unused bunk. It was quickly determined that none of us had heard Jack's return during the night, which only a deaf person would have missed, and Kent suggested that the remainder of us chow down while he searched for our missing teammate.

Kent returned to the barracks area about an hour later with a forlorn Jack, who'd spent the night in a Conex container converted into a cell by the local MPs. The pen gun distress flares we'd observed had originated from an inebriated Jack taking potshots at the MPs, and they obviously hadn't shared his playfulness. Kent's desperate pleas with the MPs had won Jack a get-out-of-jail-free card, and thus no paper trail would follow us back to English. As it stood, we'd all be lucky not to wind up in LBJ considering what we'd already pulled at Phu Cat.

I hadn't consumed an ice cream cone since the Manteca Foster's Freeze while on leave, and I decided to give the little parlor a shot. An older Vietnamese mama-san ran the place and was conversing with a young woman and her young daughter. It was readily apparent that they knew the significance of my cammie uniform and company scroll, and I detected fear in their eyes. Ordering a double scoop of vanilla, I turned with a grin to the little girl and handed her the cone. The uneasy atmosphere transformed to gaiety in an instant, and it was one of the most rewarding experiences of my life. I might not have understood a lick of Vietnamese, nor they English, but ice cream and little kids were a universal language. If only just this once, maybe I'd won three hearts and minds in this hellhole. I still see the little girl's face in my dreams and wonder what became of her. The older mama-san's name was Pham Ti Hue, and on my third and final visit to the snack bar, she presented me with a pure-gold one-and-a-half-inch Buddha figurine on a gold neck chain. Why? Because I'd given her granddaughter the ice cream cone.

The trip back to English two days later was deathly silent. Kent wrung his hands in preoccupation while cooking up a damage-control story for Phu Cat. Meanwhile, I fretted over the hell I'd pay for assaulting the gate guard. Maybe I could blame it on the Mateus.

All seemed normal as we strode through the compound archway and into our hooch. Then John stormed in. "Do you assholes realize just how much you fucked up? The base commander at Phu Cat wanted to hang all of your asses until Captain Tanaka sweet-talked him and brigade down! Just so you know, N/75 Ranger is now permanently banned from the Phu Cat NCO club thanks to you guys! And why in the hell were you guys packing weapons and frags to begin with?!"

One thing I was grateful for at that very moment was John's apparent lack of knowledge concerning the air policeman I'd popped at Phu Cat, and I crossed my fingers that the man had been too embarrassed to report it to his bosses. Had word gotten back about Jack being tossed in the bucket at China Beach, we'd really have been screwed, too. What truly made me shudder was the thought of what might have happened had Jack chosen to hide a couple of frags instead of his pen gun kit.

Captain Tanaka eventually rotated to a staff job, and as his replacement, we received Maj. William H. Shippey as our new commanding officer. Major Shippey had just completed a tour as an adviser with a Vietnamese Ranger battalion, was extremely outgoing, and knew his job and looked out for his men.

My left elbow had also taken a turn for the worse, and Doc Creamer had no choice but to send me down to B Med. "Wear sunglasses and don't turn your bad side towards the doc." I again evaded discovery, but the guy stuck my arm in a sling and profiled me light duty for a week. The duty wasn't bad as I took TOC watches and learned a lot from Sgt. Don Costello, who actually ran the place.

On another Nui Mieu mission, we'd discovered a fresh cooking fire in a dense rock formation on a steep trail paralleling a river. Knowing that we had bad guys nearby, we set up an LP at their now former campsite. I'd taken a break from point, swapping with Jack on rear security, when I observed two VC soldiers approaching my position. At about fifteen meters, I emptied a thirty-round magazine on the point man, instantly putting him down and seriously wounding the second man who fled. John blew the Claymore we'd set at rear, and I departed under Chuck's cover to check the kill zone. I was totally unprepared for the sight that greeted me. The gook I'd tagged was on his belly facing downhill on his elbows. He was wide awake and frantically screaming. In what was likely a spasmodic reaction from being hit, his left hand jerked down to his left waist where a U.S. M-67 grenade remained secured to his belt. I saw no choice but to finish him off with two rounds to the head. When I rolled him over, I counted eleven rounds in his chest area with numerous others on his arms and legs, and all I could think was that he'd either been loaded on some kind of dope or just didn't realize that he was already dead. Checking his ID, I found a snapshot of a young woman and infant male, obviously his family.

Having secured the immediate contact area and with Chuck continuing to provide my cover, I proceeded farther down the trail in search of the other guy I'd tagged. I followed a heavy blood trail approximately fifty meters leading to an abandoned AK-47. With no body present, I figured he'd just wanted to dash off to die in peace—or maybe his buddies had dragged him off. I prudently opted not to pursue the matter any further and returned to the relative safety of the team.

With the team now burdened with two captured weapons and some documents, John called for an emergency extraction because of our having been compromised. Sergeant First Class Jones was working the TOC and promptly refused the request, instead ordering us to continue the mission. John's anger was clearly evident over the commo with Jones, and this was to be the first of two identical stunts he pulled on Team Hotel.

As we moved out of the overhanging rock camp area, we began taking semi-auto Russian SKS rounds from our right flank. The two gooks I'd fired up obviously had buddies nearby, and considering the limited options available to us in this dense lower terrain, we chose to make a run for higher ground. It was another session of cat chasing mouse as we'd advance 100 meters or so, LP for a couple of minutes, then continue the dash. John smartly ordered us not to expend ammo unnecessarily as there was a better than average chance we'd really need it soon.

In a gift from heaven, we received commo from Sgt. Don Costello. Major Shippey had countermanded Jones's order, and we were to reach a nearby suitable extraction LZ as soon as possible at coordinates provided by Costello. The bird would most likely be early on station orbiting, and the accompanying gun ships could take care of any gooks dead on our asses. The gooks must have heard the inbound choppers and given up on us as we had a peaceful extraction.

Having long anticipated the event, N/75 Ranger's members finally received the black beret in an awards ceremony presided over by the brigade commander, Brig. Gen. Jack MacFarlane. Meanwhile, the good general's platoon of white ducks had long beforehand been awarded GI dog tags, maintained to a blinding sheen by an SP5 orderly.

John Kirk and Kent Farrand DEROS'd virtually together, and Dave Blow departed on extension leave. Team Hotel picked up SP4 Leroy "Jake" Dymond from Pennsylvania as our new RTO; SP4 Joseph D. "Jay" Hayes from Weed, California, packing the M-203; and SP4 Philip "Tish" Tischman from Merced, California, as our new team leader. Chuck picked up the assistant team leader slot.

On April 6, 1971, my twenty-third birthday, the company mounted a heavy mission into the Soui Ca Valley with all teams participating. Upon receiving word of the operation a few days earlier, a dark pall had fallen over the company as it was known that we'd by going in "hot" against at least an NVA battalion, possibly even a brigade. As if every mission we pulled wasn't mortally hazardous enough, the higher-ups had singled this one out, strongly suggesting that we make sure our personal affairs were in order. Did they know something we didn't?

Despite the Casper gun ships and F-4 Phantom jets from Phu Cat performing a good prep job on the LZ, the mission began badly and progressed to worse. As our insertion bird commenced touchdown, we detected the terrifying metallic rap of supersonic lead tracer rounds impacting aircraft aluminum, and with the door gunners frantically sweeping the LZ, we literally dove head first out the doors.

Exiting the aircraft alive was one thing, but here we were in an open area with no options other than to run for our lives and try to keep the gooks heads down with return fire . . . and pray that our supporting gun ships didn't tag us in all of the confusion. Personally, I was pumping out 40-millimeter high-explosive rounds from my M-79 like there'd be no tomorrow. Swamp Rat meanwhile hosed down the area with the M-60, and I prayed he wouldn't burn out the goddamned barrel.

With the gooks boldly trailing us, we'd moved about one klick through a relatively open and lightly rolling area with rice paddies bordered by thick double-canopy jungle. Team Hotel was in trail of Kilo Team on point. As they made a minor bend and rise in the trail, we heard a loud explosion accompanied by a column of dark smoke. John Hines, temporarily assigned to Kilo and on point, had tripped a rigged B-40 rocket, seriously wounding himself and his slack, George Welch. The remainder of Kilo assumed flank security while we advanced to the site to provide additional cover and aid the wounded. While John had moderately serious head wounds and a badly mangled right hand, Welch appeared to be history. Doc Creamer came forward to handle Welch while I bandaged and attempted to calm Hines. Creamer didn't think Welch was going to make it (we never found out). The gooks in the meantime had been bold enough to take potshots at the inbound dustoff bird. As it touched down, I experienced the eerie realization that I'd been here before—only instead of being the mangled guy lying on the deck, I was now watching. Most days in this place were just outright bizarre.

Continuing our movement, we engaged a small element about thirty minutes later. I'd been on point for Hotel and was trailing Dave Cummings when I saw him fire at a gook sitting against a tree. The gook had just pulled the fuze lanyard on a Chicom frag, and upon being shot, he'd dropped the frag in his lap while pitching forward. Dave yelled "Frag!" and the frag detonated, returning the gook to a sitting position. What happened next was possible only in combat. The gook's chest cavity had been blown wide open, exposing his slowly beating heart. The beating stopped, and the heart fell out of the gook's chest cavity onto his mangled legs.

Shortly after Dave's stellar performance as an on-the-job cardiac surgeon, a golden opportunity came my way on the same mission. Our team had been casually sitting on a high volcanic bluff overlooking a relatively barren valley, save one large tree about 250 meters away. Ramsland was the first to do a double-take on the tree with his exclamation of a gook standing beside it. Snatching binoculars out of my ruck, I zeroed in on the tree—and there stood a gook, probably a trail watcher, in black PJs armed with a Russian SKS rifle. Feeling playful but with my M-79 not immediately accessible, I asked to borrow Jack's M-203 and racked a white-phosphorus round. I watched the round's travel as the gook spun around to run and unbelievably observed it impact center mass of his back. He dropped his weapon and pitched face-first to the ground with his PJs in flames.

Later that afternoon, we broke off into individual teams and soon wished for the relative security of the full company. Our team had been observed from its breakup with the company and been tracked about 500 meters by a reinforced rifle platoon to an LP we'd just set up. We detected extensive movement approaching our position, accompanied by whistles and bullhorns. These yo-yos were brazenly telling us "GI, you die!"

and deploying themselves in an enveloping maneuver around us. We seriously debated dropping our rucksacks and running for it, but prudently decided to keep same as they contained all of our spare ammo, explosives, radio batteries, water, and other supplies.

We literally ran for about three hours with these people at our backs, knowing better than to stop and attempt a last stand fighting them off. The remainder of the company was in similar straits from what we could gather over the radio, and again the thought crossed our minds that this wasn't going to be our day at all. Later that evening, we initiated a hasty ambush on a much smaller element who'd stayed on our tail, and for obvious reasons, we didn't stick around to check the kill zone. This maneuver at least temporarily halted the main body's advance, enabling us to reach higher ground with much better cover and concealment.

We set up a tight wagon-wheel defensive position in thick bramble, and soon the gooks were on us with flashlights. They were close enough to grab, and I was dead sure that they could hear my heart pounding. All of us were probably anticipating a sudden light show of muzzle flashes followed by permanent lights out. And then, as fast as the little bastards had arrived, they were gone.

Swamp Rat had probably saved our bacon by being super thorough with his closing of our trail into the bramble. We slept in restless shifts for the remainder of the night, all of us on pins and needles at the slightest rustle of jungle growth or wildlife. I again thought back to earlier in the day when Hines and Welch had been hit. I'd literally come full circle, and in view of our present circumstances, I hoped that the team, along with myself, wasn't on the other way back around again.

We successfully made it to our emergency PZ the next morning, and following an uneventful extraction, we were re-inserted with the balance of the company into another portion of the Soui Ca. We learned that a relatively new member of Alpha Team, Chris Simmons, had achieved a fifty-meter headshot with an M-203 high-explosive round in near-darkness—a phenomenal feat of skill and luck. Later that morning, Team Hotel was walking point—myself with Lyons as slack man—with Kilo trailing as we negotiated a dense boulder formation.

---+----- ≡◊≡ -----+---

A muscular inflammation condition Swamp Rat had suffered intermittently since childhood had begun giving him grief, and First Sergeant Moore placed him on light support duty in the company. He'd fulfilled his dream to be a LRP and had been a definite asset to Team Hotel.

No Vietnam combat tour is complete without one's having bragging rights about surviving a typhoon. My opportunity came in mid-April with a mission in the Tiger Mountains. We were engaged in another company-strength mission, and Team Hotel had been designated for five days serving dual roles as parent-unit radio relay and security for a mortar platoon on a remote-fire support base named Maude.

The mission started out on a pleasant note. The mortar platoon guys were keeping us well fed and providing on-the-job training on their 81-millimeter and 4.2-inch toys. Our teams in the field had produced positive results with no good guys being hurt, and we almost felt as if we were on a wilderness vacation. As an added surprise, a trio of Red Cross girls was airlifted out one afternoon for a few hours of morale boosting. It goes without saying that their appearance failed to develop into anything remotely resembling our New Year's party in the Ranger Club.

On what we believed to be our last day out, the mortar platoon expended their remaining ordnance with a series of mad minutes. Naturally, Team Hotel was allowed to partake in the festivities, and in no time flat, we were yelling "Hang it!" with the best of them.

An incident on an adjacent ridgeline provided brief entertainment for all of us. A UH-1 Huey had attempted a landing on the ridge top. The guy had almost made it to touchdown when a main rotor blade struck a tree and snapped in half. We watched the rocking fuselage and gyrating main rotor mast until all came to a halt. Then as if nothing had happened, the entire crew nonchalantly exited the aircraft as if it were a taxi.

The mortar guys soon packed up their stuff and were extracted back home to English. Meanwhile, we'd been instructed to just sit tight and await word on a pull time. We'd all noted darkening skies to the west, and from my limited training in aviation meteorology, I observed what appeared to be an approaching typhoon front. We got on the horn and advised TOC of the deteriorating weather, and what we got in reply was brigade's instruction that we remain on Maude for a stay-behind ambush. After all, the gooks just loved scavenging freshly departed American defensive positions.

So here we were out in the middle of nowhere with truly fucked up weather about to hammer us, and not a Chinaman's chance for escape were we to be hit by the gooks. And the least of our problems was that the mortar guys had torn down all shelter, so we'd soon be sitting in uncovered foxholes with heavy winds and lightning on the way. We were human lightning rods—to say nothing of our long whip radio antenna— and had no protection other than our poncho liners.

Just as feared, Typhoon Wanda, as the National Weather Service had named her, hit with a vengeance, with lightning immediately taking out our Claymores and the gale force winds threatening to literally blow us all off the hilltop. Naturally, nobody other than Team Hotel could be nuts enough to be out in this shit. As darkness fell, we quickly exhausted the small supply of hand-popper parachute illumination flares the mortar guys had left us, and the radio was useless with the intense electrical activity. Nobody slept, and we spent the night cursing whoever in brigade had come up with this deal.

Upon returning to English, we were confronted with massive company area destruction from the typhoon. An exception was Hotel Hooch, which, although having lost its roof, had come through unscathed. None of our personal possessions had been damaged, including Chuck's expensive Pioneer stereo system, and even our Mateus bottles had remained unbroken in the ceiling rafters. Most of the other teams didn't fare as well, but with typical Ranger resourcefulness, we rebuilt the place within days.

Company N Ranger had experienced a number of KIAs during my tour. Sgt. George Morgan had, of course, died in a tragic grenade accident. Staff Sgt. Juan Borja and SP4 Larry Peel lost their lives fighting the enemy on April 28, 1971, along with a new member who died accidentally from a friendly booby-trap. SP4 Joe Sweeney was killed on May 29, and on June 13, Team Hotel lost Joseph D. "Jay" Hayes to close-range enemy fire while we awaited extraction on a hilltop in the Nui Mieus. Hayes was relatively new to the team, having volunteered for LRP duty from the safety and security of a clerk assignment at Cha Rang Valley.

The seven-day duration mission had produced no enemy contacts, just numerous signs of their presence—fresh sandal tracks, recently used campsites, and distant light-weapons fire, which we were told involved a line unit in contact. Call it gut instinct, sixth sense, premonition, or whatever, we all had the unshakeable feeling that we were being watched.

Our problems had actually started the night before our scheduled extraction when we detected a column of NVA moving north in a valley from the northern base of our NDP terrain feature. They were probably headed for Phu My, a known NVA assembly and supply area. We counted 325 well-armed troops before total darkness, and the individual supervising the TOC—Jones—hadn't believed us. To make matters worse, he initiated artillery fire on the coordinates we gave for the sighting. Along with the acting team leader, Stephen Joley, Team Hotel vehemently opposed this because of the high probability of the gooks putting two and two together.

The next morning, in what turned out to be yet another bad move, Jack was extracted individually for business back at English. Jones's logic was that the gooks would believe we'd all been pulled. Yeah, right: they were probably looking down our throats through binoculars as we spoke.

Hayes soon after advised that he was going to OP/LP on a trail extending from our NDP across a saddle to an adjacent hilltop. Considering the previous night's activities and a strong likelihood that the gooks had left a stay-behind force to monitor us (at a minimum), I instructed him not to go more than twenty-five meters away from the team.

The whole world went to hell in a hand basket about ten minutes after Hayes's departure: first, a short burst of AK-47 from the adjoining hilltop at an unidentified target, then the gooks started dumping on us. I yelled down the trail for Hayes and received no response. Chuck and I reached simultaneous conclusions that Hayes, sometimes too curious, had performed his own recon to the other hilltop and discovered gooks assembling to take us on. In response, Joley headed down the trail in search of Hayes while we provided covering fire and called in the contact/emergency extraction report.

Joley failed to reappear within a reasonable amount of time, and Lyons dashed off searching for him and Hayes. I broke out my M-79 in hopes of keeping the gooks' heads down while Dymond pumped out additional high explosive from his M-203. Just maybe we could provide our missing teammates a brief escape window. Now it was just Dymond and I on the NDP, and when Lyons failed to show, I figured all three of them had bought it. Considering the large number of enemy we'd observed the evening prior, I feared an encircling maneuver with an eventual uphill sweep. There'd be absolutely nowhere to run, just a replay of Custer's Last Stand. Trying to conceal my near-panic, I instructed Jake to secure the trail from which we'd entered the NDP the day before, further stating that if he were to be the only one remaining, he was to destroy the SOI and KAC wheel, then run like hell for a decent hiding place until an emergency extraction reached him.

As though he'd been resurrected from the grave, I heard Chuck loudly whispering from about fifty meters down the trail that he'd been hit in the knee and couldn't make it up the hill and that Joley and Hayes were KIA. Leaving Dymond with the radio, I literally slid down the hill to Chuck with the gooks now seemingly attracted to my open target. With sporadic rounds impacting around us, I snatched Chuck's arm, and we made it back up to the NDP in an adrenaline boost.

When Chuck had caught his breath, he stated that he had spotted Hayes on the opposite hilltop lying on his back, obviously dead. Just about then, the gooks had opened up on him and tagged him in the knee. He hadn't seen or heard Joley, and the only logical conclusion was that he too was KIA.

Jones advised that he was inbound in an Air Force 0-1 "Bird Dog" forward air controller aircraft and that a reaction platoon from Uplift was also on the way. Furthermore, Major Shippey was en route to pull Chuck for the 65th Evacuation Hospital in Qui Nhon.

The birds from LZ Uplift's 2nd 503rd Infantry reaction platoon were now fast approaching, and out of the clear blue came Joley running into the NDP. He'd been pinned down by the same gooks who'd wounded Chuck and probably killed Hayes. He had observed Chuck struggling by him during his return to the NDP. Joley had been pinned down early in the contact and thus hadn't made it to Hayes's body.

With Chuck on the way to the hospital in Major Shippey's chopper and the reaction force linked up with us, I assumed point, with Joley and Dymond trailing for the trip across the saddle to secure Jay's body. The gooks had apparently beat feet into a large draw with all of the air activity, and we made it across with only occasional harassing fire.

Having reached the military crest of the opposite terrain feature, I informed the second lieutenant who led the reaction platoon of my intent to conduct a solo probe ahead of the column. My motives were first of all to flush out any remaining gooks and then determine the location of Hayes's body. Doing so alone was based on sound tactical logic, since the last thing I'd need was a herd of elephants following me with their unavoidable noise-discipline violations. Besides, if I actually ran into something demanding a hasty retreat, a blocked trail wouldn't be beneficial to anybody. Departing the main body, I advised the platoon leader that I'd be tossing frags as bait and requested that his folks not overreact and fire. If the coast was clear, I'd fire two rounds in rapid succession signaling a linkup. If not, I'd scream like hell for help.

With my pucker factor at max, I proceeded up the trail, noting not only Jay's fresh bootprints but recent enemy sandal tracks as well. I reached the conclusion that the gooks had very possibly started for our position during the prior evening and had been scared off by the sudden friendly artillery mission in the adjacent valley.

Having received no response from my probing with the frags, I found Jay approximately seventy-five meters from our main body lying on his back as Chuck had described, with his feet pointing down the trail in our direction. What I believe happened is that he discovered the ambush, albeit too late, and had attempted to escape the kill zone. The entire back of his skull had been blown away, and I reasoned that he had been facing away from the enemy in an attempted egress when he was KIA.

Jay's body had been on the trail for the better part of an hour, and I feared that he might be booby-trapped. This was reinforced by the fact that although the gooks had taken Jay's weapon, they hadn't removed his web gear or grenades. As long as I live, I'll never forget the startled look in his eyes when I inspected his body for enemy tampering. He had to have known his number was up. While probing under Jay's head and body for pressure-release devices or a planted frag, I had the unenviable experience of his brain matter and blood spilling onto my hands and shirtsleeves. I recall feeling an intense rage and yelling at the reaction force platoon leader: "Let's go get those motherfuckers!"

Still wary over the possibility of Jay's being booby-trapped, we secured a sling rope to his ankles and dragged his body for approximately five meters. Gently wrapping Jay's lifeless form in a poncho, Team Hotel's role as a LRP team reverted to that of pallbearers as we carried him back to the NDP for our extraction. The reaction force, along with a full company inbound from English, would remain in the area hunting for our attackers.

The flight to LZ English was surrealistic, with the flight crew respectfully avoiding looking not only at Jay's body, but at us as well. Rather than proceeding directly to the crap table, the crew thoughtfully dropped us and our lifeless teammate at graves registration. Sergeant Taring in the meantime had personally driven down our company's three-quarter truck for a lift back to the hill, and we said our final good-byes to Jay.

In what began as an unexpected and happy reunion, Sgt. John Fowler, who'd shipped over with me from Fort Lewis, was on an in-country R&R from L/75 Ranger up at Phu Bai and stopped in for a visit. Naturally, the entire team joined in the festivities with ample Mateus wine being served. The 4th Battalion, 503rd, had recently threatened to conduct an assault on our company area in retaliation for hard feelings generated at the steak house, and Major Shippey wisely instituted one-man company gate guard shifts (armed with a bunk adapter and Thunderer whistle) during the hours of darkness.

Typical in units such as N/75 was a fatalistic attitude rather than the World War II–style mom's-apple-pie or girl-back-home stuff. Many members who'd served any appreciable time in the company had experienced Dear John letters, divorce papers, KIA buddies, and other troubles, and thus, extending one's tour was a stopgap defense mechanism out of the World's hassle and heartbreak. It was almost cultist, only instead of rubber heads like Charlie Manson or Anton Le Vey preaching gibberish to impressionable kids, everything made sense as long as it concerned offing the enemy or avoiding the madness stateside. Inevitably, I too fell under this spell. The letters from Cassandra had been coming on a semiregular basis, but as I'd realized earlier, we had no real future. In bold jest, I'd often tell my teammates that maybe I could track down my ex-flame Susan and her husband. In the end, all I desperately desired was to remain in-country and see the war to its conclusion, then move on to the next skirmish. If misfortune should again befall me, such was the way of things sometimes.

Word came down from brigade that the Herd would soon be rotating back to Fort Campbell under Nixon's troop withdrawal schedule. The brigade colors would then be deactivated and its personnel absorbed by the now LEG 101st Airborne Division (Airmobile). Our company, on the other hand, would retire its colors to Fort Benning with the remaining personnel spread to the four winds, depending on time remaining in country, service, and other factors. I'd earlier applied and had been approved for a six-month extension of my combat tour under "present duty assignment." Since N/75 would no longer exist, it was a literal tossup as to what I'd draw for a new unit. I put a bug in Sergeant First Class Taring's ear to try to swing me into one of the remaining Ranger companies, and he promised to look into it.

I was soon made aware of my immediate fate. Taring's efforts on my behalf had been for naught, and he handed me a set of orders reassigning me to Company A, 4th Battalion, 503rd Infantry, with a reporting date of June 25. Along with Jack Ramsland, I'd be pulling donkey security duty on the English perimeter while the brigade moved out, and then I'd be transferred to Cam Ranh Bay for security blocking force operations in the mountains west of Cam Ranh Air Base. The company was still actively running missions, and I requested a delayed reporting date to the 503rd. I was granted a "pardon" through July 10, which would allow me at least two more missions with the team.

My last mission with Team Hotel ended with our touchdown on the crap table during the afternoon of July 9. A final bash in the Ranger Club, one last night in Hotel hooch, and it was over. I was choked with emotion the next morning in anticipation of the good-byes to follow. Aside from my teammates, I bade farewell to such outstanding guys as Major Shippey, Top Moore, Sergeant First Class Taring, Dave Cummings, Mike Hines, Ron Wafer, Gordon Baker, Rudy Teodosio,

Mike Arredondo, Sven and Robert Henriksen ("The Twins")—
the list was almost endless. With my bags and orders for the
Bronze Star and Air Medal in hand, I passed through the
Ranger archway for the last time, bound for what would prove
to be a brief hell on earth. I had run about thirty-one missions
with N/75 Ranger.

As for our company mascots, Tango and Bullet, I never
learned Bullet's fate. I later heard that one of our guys had
completed the paperwork to take Tango home, but through an
administrative screw-up, the MPs had put Tango down, which
really stirred up some shit.

From the first second Jack and I stepped into the flapped
door of Company A's 3rd Platoon tent, we hated the place. The
counterculture attitude prevailed, and Jack and I made a decision then and there to avoid these people as much as practical.
We never met our company commander or platoon leader, and
the platoon sergeant was so harried with disciplinary problems
that he didn't know night from day. The weapons and equipment were for the most part in states of disrepair or just plain
worn out, and we prayed this wouldn't last long.

We were immediately assigned to swing-shift perimeter
security—believe me that after eight hours of peering through
a Starlight scope, I was probably seeing as many hallucinations
as the acid heads. In one golden opportunity, I dropped a
final gook with the Herd. It was late evening, and I'd been
scanning the village of Di Duc, located on the western English
perimeter, when I detected a lone armed form in a rice paddy
about 300 meters away. Summoning the officer-in-charge, a
major, for advice, he quickly confirmed the sighting and called
for 4.2 mortar illumination rounds. "He's all yours, Walker." I
had a scoped and well-zeroed M-14 available for just such a
"target of opportunity," and when the lights went on, I
dropped the gook like he was pole-axed. The shot generated
numerous catcalls and laughs, which suited my presently
depressed persona just fine. This elite assignment lasted for
two weeks, after which the company transferred to Cam Ranh
Bay to secure the brigade's departure.

The C-123 trip from LZ English to Cam Ranh Bay wasn't without its entertainment. Shortly after takeoff, the copilot, obviously suffering a crippling hangover, exited the cockpit for a piss break. Staggering down the center aisle for the aft piss tube, the guy lost his lunch and took a dive face-first to the cabin floor. Despite the poor soul pissing himself, the loadmaster, to his credit, laid his incapacitated fellow crew member on the troop seat and strapped him down for a short sleep. The crew chief meanwhile jumped into the copilot's seat to turn the knobs for the aircraft commander. It went without saying that what we'd witnessed stayed in the aircraft. I mean, who were we to point fingers about anything, considering the stunts we'd pulled?

For the next two weeks, we lived in an immense boulder formation about three klicks west of the airport. Up and down, back and forth—make sure there aren't any gooks behind that rock.

One of the first things Jack and I learned about the line units was that other than the drugs, they lived an extremely dangerous lifestyle from a tactical standpoint. Here were guys cooking their chow in the middle of the night with C-4 and playing heavy metal on their boom boxes. Complacency prevailed, and there was virtually no effective guard duty at night. Most of the guard posts slept, stayed stoned, or both. In one especially harrowing incident, a young private first class on a local patrol I had been leading left cover to climb a large boulder. Why? He wanted to perform his impression of Elvis Presley before his buddies, using his M-16 for a guitar. I went ballistic, telling everyone that every gook in the county was probably watching our every move and that it was never too late to become a KIA. Jack and I wisely separated ourselves from these suicidal maniacs at every opportunity, especially at night.

As if to prove to itself that the country could still take me out, on my very last day of pulling security in the western mountains of Cam Ranh Bay, I was nearly killed by friendly fire. A 155-millimeter howitzer battery down on the coast near the air base had fired a routine H&I mission, supposedly past our position in the western rocks. I heard a round fly over my position with the usual *whoosh,* with a distant *crunch* detonation. A split second later, a disc-shaped chunk of shrapnel about five-by-seven inches struck a hardwood tree I was parked next to, after which it buzz-sawed itself vertically along the trunk down to my right side with a loud *thud.* I incredulously gawked at the smoking thing and mindlessly picked it up, painfully scorching my fingers. The ugly and deadly piece of junk had missed my head by a mere six inches. And I still had to come back to this place?

Along with promotion orders to sergeant, I soon received ICT orders for the 23rd Infantry Division (American), my first ever LEG infantry assignment. They stated a reporting date of September 9, following a thirty-day extension leave to the States.

CHAPTER 11

Final Months in Vietnam

Other than stops at Kadena Air Base in Okinawa and at Anchorage, Alaska, I slept during the entire Flying Tigers DC-8 trip to McChord Air Force Base, Washington. We were trucked to nearby Fort Lewis in the middle of the night for uniform issue and a complimentary steak dinner, the closest to a "welcome home" we received. The steak could just as well have served as a chopper pilot's breast armor plate.

Arriving at San Francisco–Oakland a few hours later from SEATAC, I called Dad for a pickup. Bursting into tears, Dad sobbed: "Wizzo, why didn't you write me that you were coming home?" "No sweat, Dad. I'll be in the main terminal cocktail lounge. I love you." By the time Dad merrily strolled into the place, I was already pretty sideways.

Dad suggested that we grab a bite to eat somewhere, and I countered that we go get the girls and party at Blum's, a world-famous restaurant and lounge in the Mission District. Our family had frequented the place since Gary and I were little kids.

Still in shock over my being home, Dad asked where my new duty station would be. I told him I extended my tour and had to be back in Vietnam in thirty days. Whatever thoughts or fears Dad might have harbored, he admirably withheld them for my benefit. All he said was "I love you son, and I'm proud of what you're doing."

Although I hadn't maintained any false illusions over my relationship with Cassandra, it was genuinely comforting to see her again. Shelley was also overjoyed to see me, and the four of us lived life for a couple of days.

Earlier, Dad had depressingly revealed that Mom married some joker named Al Williams. He hadn't yet met Al, but from

the little information Mom had volunteered, the guy owned a
tire shop in West Manteca. "Okay Dad. I have to head out and
see Mom and Gary anyway, and I'll give you a SITREP when I
get back to the city."

I'd decided to catch Gary first for some intel on Al. Meeting my new sister-in-law Linda for the first time was somewhat
awkward. I'd arrived at Gary's place drunk and with a chip on
my shoulder about Al, and being fresh out of Vietnam, I
sensed Linda was afraid of me—probably with just cause.

I wasn't the least bit reassured over Gary's comments
regarding Al. We jumped in my Roadrunner and headed Code
3 for a visit with my new stepfather. Mom was initially overjoyed to see me until I brought up the subject of her new husband and his treatment of her. "Honey, please don't start any
trouble with Al or Tim." Although I'd promised Mom to maintain my cool, Al's defiant glare when I marched into his shop
instantly had me seeing red.

I apologized to Mom who by then had freaked out, and
had Gary take me to Stockton Airport. I needed to get up to
Weed, California, to visit Jay Hayes's family. I was working
myself into a state of rage over the culture shock of not only
what had happened to my family, but the demons invading my
sleep at night.

Jay's sister Helen Blevins was overjoyed to meet me, as were
the Blankenships who had treated Jay as a son. The Blankenships' older son Malcolm ("Wade") was an Army major with
the Joint Uniformed Services Military Advisory Group in Thai-
land, and we'd begin a long correspondence upon my return
in-country.

The leave was pretty much a blur of motel rooms, cocktail
lounges, taxi rides, airports, and bus terminals. Nowhere in
particular to go or people to see, just had to keep moving. I visited Chuck Lyons for a couple of days in Kendrick, Idaho, and
Gordy Baker in Mechanicsville, Iowa, then flew out to Chicago
just to see what the place was like. In one particular Italian-
owned restaurant and bar, I was unable to buy a drink.

After farewells with Gary and Mom, I headed back to San Francisco for a last bash with Dad and the girls. We saw the movie *Vanishing Point* at the San Bruno Bayshore Drive-In, and the next morning, I was en route back to Vietnam. My last glimpse of Dad alive was of he and the girls blind waving farewell from the Pan Am gate picture window as the aircraft pushed back, bound for Honolulu, Guam, and Saigon.

I reported to the 23rd Infantry Division's I Corps Happy Valley rear area west of Chu Lai on September 9. In a stroke of luck, I was briefly reunited with Sgt. 1st Class George "Cool Bru" Brubaker from my 101st Recondo School training cadre and F/58 LRP service. Bru was involved in some variety of top-secret spook stuff with MACV and was roaming the division area with an old acquaintance who just happened to be the former sergeant major of the Vietnamese Airborne School at Tan Son Nhut Air Base in Saigon. I took a shot in the dark and asked the sergeant major if he might wangle me a slot for earning ARVN parachutist wings.

With sufficient juice provided by Bru and his buddy, I was granted a five-day pass from the Happy Valley folks and headed south for Tan Son Nhut Air Base. The instruction I received at a little satellite area on the air base named Camp Ap Don was obviously abbreviated in nature, with the first day being devoted to familiarization with French jump equipment, jump commands, and other basics. On the second day, I executed three jumps, two from Vietnamese Air Force Douglas C-47 Gooney Birds and one from a De Havilland C-7A Caribou blast. All went well, with the exception of the French parachute's opening shock, which totally—and unexpectedly—jerked my pucker string loose. For my minor toils, I was presented with a very elaborate completion certificate and a photo ID. The only portions I could read—everything else was in Vietnamese—were the date and my name/rank line, but who was bitching.

As an ICT, I was spared the usual jungle-school stuff and was quickly sent north to the 196th Light Infantry Brigade ("Chargers") at Freedom Hill, Da Nang. Further assigned to Company E, 3rd Battalion, 21st Infantry ("Gimlets"), at Camp Reasoner, I was instantly policed up by 1st Lt. Thomas A. Smith, the Recon Platoon leader. Lieutenant Smith, or "Smitty" as he preferred to be addressed by his NCOs, was himself a former NCO and combat vet turned officer. We immediately hit it off, as was also the case with Staff Sgt. Dave Smith, the platoon sergeant, and First Sergeant Yeast. The company commander, Captain Steele, was seldom seen or heard, while the battalion's commander, Lt. Col. Rocco Negris, was a good guy, as was the brigade commander, Brig. Gen. Joseph McDonough.

Smitty assigned me as a recon squad leader and provided a rundown on the unit's operations. The gooks in the area were for the most part avoiding contact in consideration of not only the U.S. troop reductions, but also their buildup for the 1972 Easter Offensive. The platoon's primary job was detecting and preventing infiltration of the areas still populated by U.S. troops and remaining 23rd Division interests through area reconnaissance. These areas consisted of the immediate Hoi An Province, working north, south, and west to locales such as Quang Nai, the A Shau Valley, Antenna Valley, Que Son Valley, LZs Baldy and Mary Ann, and all Central Highland areas to the Laotian border, specifically Ho Chi Minh trail branches. The average mission lasted fourteen days with a three- or four-day recovery in between, which wasn't bad. We also held duty-exemption status, which eliminated all of the chicken shit like bunker guard. The hooches at Camp Reasoner, a former Marine Recon home, were exceptional by in-country standards. As at LZ English, the brigade had its own steak house with food of about the same quality. The NCO club, in its sincere attempt to reflect the good life for its patrons, was crammed with plastic ferns and palm trees. Nothing but the best cheap-charlie stuff for the fighting troops.

From my first view of the Da Nang area, I'd noted its striking beauty. Seemingly endless rows of rice paddies lay to the northeast through to the southeast of Camp Reasoner. Situated at the southern base of Hai Van Pass on Highway QL-1 was a Buddhist temple with an immense white Buddha statue atop the roof. The place was lit with floodlights during the hours of darkness and was truly a sight to behold. Also located to the north and south, respectively, of Da Nang Air Base were Monkey Mountain with its classified radio research site and Marble Mountain, which sheltered an inner ancient temple of worship.

The next day, I found myself at FSB Linda (Hill 350), a prominent terrain feature about two klicks west of Charlie Ridge. We caught a flight of Hueys for an insertion approximately ten klicks south of Linda. The planned ten-day mission was a simple zigzag recon back to Linda, whereupon we'd be lifted back to Reasoner.

The mission began on a tragic note with an accidental fatality. One of those notorious V-40 "mini baseball" frags had snagged its oversized safety pin lanyard on brush and killed a young private first class. Through miscommunication, the casualty had been called in as WIA rather than KIA, a situation that generated a heated argument between the evacuation pilot and me. Upon noting a fatality rather than wounded casualty aboard his aircraft, the aircraft commander told me me he wasn't geared for KIAs. Naturally, every gook in town now knew our position Not a good way to begin a new tour. Consequently, we were pulled and moved to the opposite side of our box to begin the recon.

A dangerous item I'd immediately noted about the platoon was that battalion headquarters ran it like a standard line infantry unit. Well, the line doggies routinely fielded more than 100 men while we had 23 on a good day, and we penetrated much farther into no-man's-land. I politely mentioned this to Smitty and Dave, who hilariously replied in unison that if I thought things were raggedy now, I should have seen them a few months ago. For example, up until recently, the guys had intentionally observed poor light and noise discipline on missions. Why? Because some loony dopehead from a line company had told them that doing so would scare off the gooks.

Once again, the old false sense of security in numbers mani-
fested itself. Reassuring were Smitty and Dave's comments of
our having an excellent talent pool of combat vets to draw
from. They just needed a little motivation. The sad state of
affairs in the platoon was in no way due to a lack of leadership
on the parts of Smitty and Dave. As previously stated, we'd
been misused by battalion headquarters and had recently
experienced a relatively high turnover rate through members
completing their tours; as such, we had played a constant
game of catch-up with training.

Things smoothed out somewhat over the next few days at
Camp Reasoner. Unlike strictly volunteer units I'd served in
before, the majority of 196th soldiers were draftees. Not that
this made them any less capable than the elite volunteers, but
there was a mood of "I don't want to be the last GI killed in
Vietnam." For that matter, neither did I, but my fear was over
the war ending before I'd sated myself to the point of either
boredom or exhaustion. Whatever the case, these people
needed to acquire combat-survival skills in a hurry to help keep
me alive, too.

Fortunately, the Recon Platoon, although not truly a volunteer outfit, had been blessed with a small number of elite
unit veterans and higher-caliber low rankers. With their help, I
wanted to transform the main body into gung-ho active enemy
pursuers, rather than soldiers who just sat in an OP reading
Playboy while the gooks waltzed merrily by pacifist American
GIs. Some of these guys had been in-country for months and
had yet to be exposed to hostile fire. I'd just as soon get their
cherries busted now than learn some ugly truths during a desperate situation.

With Smitty's blessing, Dave, our other experienced vets,
and I commenced a crash training course for the platoon.
First, these guys had to know and take pride in who they really
were. The 3/21st Recon Platoon was the only unit in the battalion authorized to wear the jungle camouflage uniform, even
in the rear area. A visit to the local gook seamstress produced
red and blue "3 RECON 21" scrolls for rear-area cammies—a

real morale booster and excellent profile shot at the brigade enlisted men and NCO clubs. Two other great morale boosters were our platoon mascot puppies, Claymore and Bullet.

The low rankers were sorely lacking elementary skills in map reading, radio procedure, artillery adjustment, booby-trap construction and detection—the list was endless. Hell, the poor guys couldn't even pack a ruck or apply camo stick correctly. With the basics out of the way, more attention could be devoted to other vital skills such as silent movement, light and noise discipline, IA drills, and others.

Slowly but surely, even troops who had only recently been considered "duds" began shaping up, and personally, my confidence factor for these guys *not* getting me killed went up tenfold. Top Yeast and Captain Steele were ecstatic over the drastically reduced discipline problems.

I had never taken advantage of the two out-of country R&Rs I was authorized with my normal tour and extension. To my dismay, Top Yeast informed me that the out-of-country R&R program had been cancelled during mid-1971, but he offered me five days at China Beach or Vung Tau. I had already made the China Beach scene, and although it was nice enough, things just wouldn't be the same without my Hotel teammates.

Vung Tau turned out to be a real dream come true, with ample exotic bars, plenty of women, and good chow, not to mention the Australian SAS and their regular army guys based there to party with. I'd never had the opportunity to sample the Vietnamese beers Tiger ("Panther Piss") and Ba-Mi-Ba 33, both loaded with formaldehyde and guaranteed to create a murderous hangover. The downside of playing in the South China Sea was the killer cross-current a short distance from the shoreline, and I wisely stayed out of the water when inebriated. Totally bizarre were the U.S. Army Special Services (not to be confused with Special Forces)—lifeguards, surfboards, and even fishing boat trips. On my last day of R&R, I purchased a stuffed mongoose attacking a cobra diorama, which was promptly stolen upon my return to Camp Reasoner.

The Recon Platoon endured the wrath of Typhoon Hester during the month of October during our dismantling of FSB Mary Ann. Mary Ann had been the site of a recent disastrous overrunning by gooks in the middle of the night. The security had been totally lax, and a load of heavy brass were relieved of command over that deal. We'd all been severely deprived of sleep because of the inclement weather, and our platoon medic, SP4 Robert J. "Doc" Boyden, provided us with his brand of artificial alertness (legal army speed) known as "Doc Boyden's Get-Up-'n'-Go Pills." In total oblivion to the torrential downpour and high-velocity winds hammering us, we jovially sang the song "Raindrops Keep Falling on My Head" throughout the night's unrelenting downpour. The platoon had been assigned as perimeter security outside the wire, and rather than maintaining a vigil for gooks who certainly weren't stupid enough to be wandering around in this shit, it was all we could do to prevent sliding down the hill's 45 percent grade. The solution was to plant a boot against a tree stump and maintain your balance—and forget about sleeping.

By morning, the weather had marginally improved, and none of us were prepared for the spectacle we were about to witness. A CH-54 Sky Crane heavy-lift helicopter had been dispatched from Da Nang with a sling-loaded Caterpillar D-9 bulldozer, which would level the remaining firebase structures and destroy dug-in defensive positions, thus rendering the place useless to the gooks. With the D-9 suspended precariously about 200 feet above the deactivated TOC, a gust of wind came up and caused the D-9 to begin a pendular motion under the aircraft. As if that weren't bad enough, the thing started pinwheeling on the sling. The crew chief sling operator sitting in his "telephone booth" lower observation bubble immediately figured out that something was drastically wrong and released the load directly over the TOC. The fall naturally rendered the dozer useless, missing a five-man work crew by mere feet. The basically unarmed chopper made a rapid departure from the area without so much as a token apology from what we heard. Only in Vietnam.

Staff Sgt. Dave Smith from Detroit and I became especially close friends, and in a well-fueled ceremony one evening at our local NCO club, we became blood brothers through pricking our index fingertips and joining them. This ritual was repeated on more than one occasion in case the first hadn't taken. Following one such reaffirmation, Dave and I were crossing a rickety footbridge overlooking a sewage drainage trench. Staggering, I managed to break through the handrail and take a twenty-foot free fall into the mess. Other than a funky uniform, I was unscratched. In a well-received act of compassion over my shitty swan dive, Dave swore to keep mum on my impromptu debut as a Hollywood stuntman.

Unlike N/75 Ranger, the missions were usually monotonous and seemed to run together. A memorable contact with a small NVA force occurred in an area named Bouk, located due west at the halfway point between Da Nang and the Laotian border. We had discovered a fresh cooking fire and a fairly extensive underground hospital complex with nobody home. SP4 Rex W. "Bones" Hall, a Special Forces B-36 LRRP veteran and close friend, was the first to detect movement down a trail leading to a large valley. Bones was a Native American from Wilmington, North Carolina, and had grown up in the wilds— I trusted his instincts. We'd made about 200 meters down the trail when we received AK fire from a semi-open and level area to our left flank. Bones launched a couple of M-79 high-explosive rounds while I maneuvered to the enemy's left flank. It was then that I spotted a dead NVA soldier lying in the open and another crawling away on all fours, still armed with his AK. I yelled for the guy to halt, and instead, he spun around leveling his weapon on me. It wasn't even a contest. The first gook we spotted turned out to be an NVA doctor complete with a well-stocked aid bag. The one I tagged was a lieutenant, his pockets stuffed with maps and other documents the military intelligence folks would love. Further inspection of the area revealed a major NVA field hospital in a natural cave within a large boulder formation, complete with operating tables, vehicle battery–powered lighting, the whole bit. Continued sweeping of the area yielded two additional enemy KIA (armed) along with a wounded POW. Not bad for a day's work.

Captain Steele and Smitty were obviously happy with our recent productivity, and the platoon was awarded a two-day winding down at nearby Red Beach—barbecued steaks and chicken, all the booze and beer we could put down, and an old black-and-white TV to watch reruns of *The Naked City* and *The Honeymooners* broadcast on AFVN-TV.

On another local patrol off the western tip of Charlie Ridge, I was walking point—as I preferred—uphill in a densely forested area when my slack man Bones Hall abruptly grabbed my pistol belt and yanked me backwards. "Snake!" In response to my wondering facial expression, he gestured to the dark-green forest cobra making its egress very close to where I'd been standing. Bones's lightning-quick reflexes had probably saved my life or at the very least prevented my becoming deathly ill and evacuated stateside.

As with all major units in VN, drugs were a moderate problem, and to my utter shock and dismay, they'd infiltrated the Recon Platoon. One man I had previously trusted had been using heroin for an undetermined period, and nobody had detected it. He'd always performed well in the bush, and I never observed the telltale dilated pupils or drowsiness. I uncovered his use on a local mission when I discovered an empty vial on the ground in his assigned LP area. Immediately going ballistic, I placed the muzzle of my weapon against his forehead and without mincing words informed him that I should blow his brains out. Smitty and Dave overheard the confrontation and made a beeline to the position, probably saving me from a murder rap.

Back at Camp Reasoner later that evening, the first order of business was a shakedown of the entire platoon for drugs and a stern warning to come clean if anyone had a problem. The shakedown turned up nothing. Afterwards, Smitty, Dave, and I held a brief conference about the offender's fate. Having cooled off, I suggested that he be ordered to the Army Alcohol and Drug Abuse Division program ("Dope Academy") at nearby Red Beach to dry out. He was an otherwise good kid who'd fallen in with the wrong crowd of REMFs. Therefore, compelling his exposure to know-it-all counselors and filling sandbags for three weeks was sure as hell a better alternative to court-martial proceedings. The soldier heartily concurred and completed the program, later returning to duty with no further problems.

Missions originating from and operating in the local area of FB Linda were hazardous at best—not only because of the potential for running into gooks, but also because of lack of communication and carelessness. We had been sitting in an OP/LP site about half a klick south of Linda when large-caliber slugs, then heavy machine-gun reports, began impacting dangerously close to our position. Naturally, Smitty and the rest of us believed that the gooks had somehow zeroed in on our position with a Russian .51-caliber heavy machine gun. As it turned out, somebody up on Linda had decided that having a mad minute with the .50 would be loads of fun, only word hadn't been passed that we were in their direct line of fire. The same principle applied to re-entering the FB from the bush, especially at night. There was always somebody on the perimeter who hadn't received word of an inbound patrol, and this had caused friendly injuries and even fatalities in the past.

A related problem sometimes emerged with night OP patrols monitoring the extensive network of rice paddy dikes immediately north of Camp Reasoner. We'd have a five-man patrol in position on a dike for the night, and a well-meaning but errant night area security chopper pilot would mistake our guys for gooks and spotlight them with one of those 20,000 candlepower xenon deals—or worse, fire them up. It was the same old curse: lack of communication and coordination. A much less frequent but nevertheless real hazard was the cobra infestation during the rice harvest season, which was even more dangerous at night. We all knew that bamboo stalks didn't exist on paddy dikes, and a point man's detection of a dim, hooded, upright object swaying and hissing was ample reason to freeze in place. Just give the little guy right-of-way during his nocturnal hunt for chow.

The local natives employed water buffaloes as the motive means for their rice cultivation plows, and PFC Bobby Hoffman chose to dust one during a local afternoon patrol with an M-203 high-explosive round, which hit the poor thing broadside. For a few seconds afterward, obviously not yet realizing itself to be dead, the animal just stood staring at us. The fatally wounded buffalo then collapsed with a few dying grunts. Instantly seeing red, I screamed at Hoffman. These were the same people who gave us haircuts and did our laundry, and he just gave them a reason to slip with a razor or contaminate our food and water—the possibilities were endless. Smitty later informed me that the Army had paid the buffalo's owners an unspecified amount in piasters.

As if the Recon Platoon couldn't do enough to jeopardize relations with the locals, the neighboring line doggies took their sport in launching 40-millimeter CS rounds into clustered farmers. Blinded and otherwise incapacitated by the irritating gas, the gooks tripped and fell into the filthy feces-ridden paddy water. What I'd long beforehand learned in this place was that a kid could get away with what back in the World would have been a felony.

Life in Vietnam was always full of surprises, and of all the situations in which to achieve an enemy kill, one encountered by an SP4 company clerk from the 1/46 IN really took the cake. The unarmed kid had been returning in darkness from Freedom Hill PX in the company jeep when he spotted an armed VC soldier in the open attempting to cross the road. Just about when the gook had drawn a bead with his SKS, the kid made a split-second decision and put the pedal to the metal, running over the little SOB. For his quick thinking, the young man justly received an Army Commendation Medal with V-for-valor device. A kill was a kill however you logged it, and the clerk would have honest boasting rights back in the

World instead of having to meekly state he'd merely pushed a pencil in Vietnam.

Before I'd realized it, the middle of December was upon us, and I'd been in the unit for three months. Along with my buddies, I'd been anticipating another Christmas and New Year in Vietnam and noted with minor sadness that I hadn't heard from Cassandra for quite a while. I'd never entertained any expectations of having a life together. She was a free spirit and had chosen a lifestyle to match, which would have been unacceptable to me in the long run.

Smitty reluctantly detailed me as temporary cadre in Camp Reasoner's newly formed in-house 196th Light Infantry Brigade Leadership School as a weapons instructor. I asked him whether this was a reward, a punishment, or what? Was I going to be some kind of on-the-job-training Boys Town counselor? The school was intended for senior E-4s and junior E-5s who had shown promise in their units but were lacking some military skills. I was initially shocked by the volume of junior sergeants who couldn't properly break down, much less reassemble, the .45 service auto, M-60, and M-2 .50-cal machine gun. As for the elementary skill of setting battle sight zero for the M-16, forget it. Fellow instructors in other subjects had similar impressions of the students. Wasn't stateside training teaching these people anything? Most of them seemed intelligent enough. I made a two-week contribution to the brigade's junior NCOs' proficiency, which I felt to be enough, and I told Smitty I was ready to come home.

During a morning formation at Camp Reasoner on the fourteenth, Top Yeast requested my presence in the orderly room. "Sergeant Walker, I have some bad news. We just received word from the Red Cross that your dad had a major heart attack and is in the San Francisco VA hospital. I've already picked up your gear and weapon, and I'll watch them while you're gone. I have your emergency-leave orders, so go pack and I'll run you down to the airbase."

Despite my making it crystal clear to the Air Force staff sergeant ATCO representative that I was on emergency leave with my dad dying or even possibly dead, he found it necessary to hard-time me with his bureaucratic horseshit. I wasn't even ready for this jerking around and told the guy in no uncertain terms that if he didn't get me on the next plane stateside, I'd jump across the counter and run over him like a Mack truck. He finally chose to see it my way while the pilot standing next to me just looked embarrassingly away from the confrontation.

The DC-8 bound for McChord Air Force Base, Washington, wasn't due to depart for several hours, so I parked myself in the base NCO club and proceeded to self-medicate. The bartender was aware of my circumstances, and with his and another kindly Air Force sergeant's assistance, I successfully made boarding time.

I was back in Manteca and at Mom's house in less than twenty-four hours. Dad had died on the sixth, and I was overwhelmed with guilt. Of no help was Al's having forbade Mom to attend Dad's services in San Francisco. Luckily for Al, he hadn't been at home upon my arrival.

The one positive note of the unforeseen trip was meeting my newborn niece, Sherry Ann. She was the spitting image of Gary, with blonde hair and blue eyes. Gary filled me in on the particulars of Dad's passing. Like the tough guy he was, he'd experienced and survived a major heart attack, even driving himself to the VA hospital. According to the attending physician, Dad had fought a hard battle on the table, but they'd finally lost him due to a major post-operative stroke.

Dad had always loved southern California, having spent much of his young manhood there, and I accompanied his remains to Sawtelle Veterans Cemetery (now Los Angeles National Cemetery) in Santa Monica. I immediately ran into a snag with the grounds director's notification that Dad's graveside service was to be manned by the Veterans of Foreign Wars. I hadn't in the least forgotten about my first and only experience with the VFW in 1968, and I told the director that the VFW wasn't going to get within a country mile of Dad's remains. The director, who had been a B-17 waist gunner in World War II, was genuinely sympathetic to my wishes, and after a couple of phone calls, a proper detail of local Army National Guard folks was dispatched. Dad received his proper twenty-one-gun salute, and I proudly accepted his casket flag. I tossed a handful of sacred dirt on the casket and rendered a final salute to this sweet man who had given me life. (Some nineteen years later, the VFW and I settled our differences, and I became a life member.)

Christmas and New Years came and went with hardly a notice as I wandered aimlessly through California blowing dough on motel rooms and in cocktail lounges. I simply felt as if I were on a different planet than I'd known as a young kid.

Smitty and Top Yeast couldn't believe that I'd arrived back in-country. The 196th was scheduled to be deactivated in a matter of months and would be the last ground-maneuver combat unit to leave Vietnam. Comically, they both figured I'd been reassigned stateside. Not yet for this kid! Still in a cloud over Dad's death, I figured the best way out was to get back with the program as soon as possible.

The platoon had been steadily improving during my absence, and a welcome diversion during the missions was the Eagle Flights. These amounted to "shock and awe" operations into suspected enemy positions and were occasionally productive. One flight in particular into the A Shau Valley yielded an NVA company in the open on a Ho Chi Minh trail branch. Just sit in the door and pump ordnance at the gooks while the aircrew took your stick for a roller coaster ride. During one especially exciting and rewarding flight, we took out an estimated NVA reinforced rifle platoon in the open—without even having to land. Of course, our Cobra gun ships did most of the work. The downside, of course, was that we were totally exposed to ground fire. The pilots at least had armored seats, and the entire flight crew wore "chicken plates" as token protection. Despite this, the best part was that we didn't have to hump the kick-ass terrain, exhausted and wary of whatever might turn up around the next bend in the trail.

An Eagle Flight into the LZ Baldy area one afternoon proved especially hair-raising—my only ever near-crash. Intel had it that a suspected NVA platoon had taken over the long-abandoned Baldy as a temporary staging area for their upcoming Easter Offensive We had departed Camp Reasoner in a four-ship lift and had thus far experienced an uneventful and scenic ride to the Baldy area. Just about when the mountain was clearly in sight, two loud impacts in the overhead engine compartment occurred with an accompanying change in engine note. Hearing the *whoop-whoop* of the master caution klaxon, my instantly attentive gaze was directed to the instrument panel "Christmas tree" and its winking caution lights. Through discussions back in the World with my flight instructor, Dick Bridgeford, I knew that turbine engines and foreign object damage were almost always a catastrophic combination. The damage, as it turned out, had been two Russian .51-cal heavy machine-gun rounds, and as our stick held on for dear life and in terrified anticipation of catching .51 slugs in our asses, the aircraft commander, to his credit, nursed the bird as far as practical from the .51 site and executed probably the most skilled autorotation and safe emergency landing in history.

With the initial anxiety subsiding, we rapidly disembarked to set up some semblance of security around the bird. The pilot, totally pissed off, jumped out of the cockpit, threw his helmet to the ground, and to no one in particular screamed, "Son of a goddamned bitch!" Despite the circumstances, I couldn't contain a laugh, which only further angered the pilot and created a gleeful chain reaction with the other personnel, including his crew. "Fuck all you bastards! Do you know how much paperwork this shit is going to create for me?"

Our accompanying gun ships meanwhile had established a low orbit around our position while the other three lift birds dropped off the remaining sticks nearby to provide additional security. When it was determined that we were in no imminent danger of being hit, one gunship remained on station while the other departed in an attempt to bait the .51 crew. We soon heard the telltale but brief bark of a nearby .51 that had gotten off about three rounds, immediately followed by the throaty roar of the gunship's 7.62-millimeter miniguns and 2.75-inch rockets.

The gooks did in fact have a contingency in the area, and we experienced unenthusiastic incoming light-weapons fire and a few blindly shot 82-millimeter mortar rounds. We responded in kind, and the exchange was almost fun, with no known casualties on either side. When our overhead gunship departed station in the direction of the gooks, they must have seen the light and headed for whatever hiding places they'd slapped together. The platoon remained with our downed Huey until a CH-47 Chinook cargo/personnel chopper with additional gunship support appeared to sling-load the disabled bird back to Camp Reasoner. Considering the afternoon's developments, our mission was cancelled and a flight of four lift Hueys policed us up along with the chopper crew. All in all, it had been a different and even entertaining experience, with the added bonus of some cherries being busted in the platoon.

Some missions took us much farther west. Not to say that we set foot in Laos, but our toes were probably touching the borderline, and we'd been issued cross-border map sheets in the interest of not getting lost. Most interesting were the Russian T-34 tank and truck convoys we observed moving along the primary trail and its arteries. The gooks weren't even fooling around forming up for their 1972 Easter Offensive.

Most amazing for all of us—and a true reality check—was the resourcefulness and mission dedication of the gooks. Here they'd be getting the daylights pounded out of them, and hours later, they'd have detours cut to move along their merry ways once again. The heavy loads they packed—often on bicycles for crying out loud—were unbelievable as were the countless other hardships they endured. It goes without saying that these sightings were non-engagement proposals on our part— just let the F-4 jets from Da Nang Air Base handle them. Better was the AC-130 Spectre gun ship with its three 20-millimeter

Vulcan cannons and 105-millimeter howitzer, an unquestioned pee-bringer. Best yet, when a truly heavy concentration of gooks existed, the B-52 Arc Light missions with their 700- and 1,000-pound carpet bombing really stole the show.

I'd made up my mind in N/75 to remain in-country for the remainder of the war if possible. As far as I was concerned, there wasn't much to go home to: no welcome-home parades, no girl waiting, only chickenshit stateside duty. Consequently, I applied for and was denied another extension. As the battalion's command sergeant major diplomatically put it, he'd received word that I was allegedly being careless and overly aggressive in the bush, which was probably true. A last-ditch audience with our battalion commander, Lieutenant Colonel Negris, began and ended with his politely stating that he could just as easily immediately put me on a plane back to the states considering my medical profile. Now that humbled me!

One thing I'd never done was a ladder insertion from a CH-47 helicopter. The platoon was assigned an afternoon Eagle Flight to the Que Son Valley area about thirty klicks west-southwest of Da Nang, and when I had a chance to scan the area-of-operations map, I almost defecated in my pants. The assigned area of operations was on the western border of the "valley," basically all dense mountains. And these clowns expected us to infil down a sixty-foot three-eighths-inch coaxial cable and aluminum ladder whipping wildly in the rear rotor's downwash? In full combat gear? Hell, rappelling would be much safer, only hardly anybody in the outfit knew how to rappel. I asked Smitty what was the deal with our normal Huey assets, and he angrily stated that a headquarters weenie had come up with this as a way to economize our air assets.

The insertion didn't go nearly as badly as I'd envisioned, and descending the ladder, which was deployed over the open tailgate, was actually a lot of fun. Our afternoon-long nature hike yielded only tired troops. Oh, and I nearly killed myself. We had established an OP/LP site, and being the shit-hot explosives man I knew myself to be, I proceeded to set up an electrical Claymore "widow maker." All went well until a heavy downpour began, and as I connected the Starlight battery, the goddamned thing blew for no apparent reason. I'd always observed a strict policy of *never* connecting a power source to an electrical explosive device until all other steps had been completed and I had set up at a safe distance. Consequently, all I experienced was a good scare. I had apparently shaved a hair too much plastic from the C-ration spoon insulators I'd fabricated, and the current arced clean through the plastic, the circuit most likely having been completed through water contamination. Maybe somebody was trying to tell me something. Needless to say, I didn't hear the end of that incompetent display for days.

When the bird arrived for our pickup, we all learned the true definition of physical exertion. In other words, ascending the ladder was a total bitch, especially for the last person—me!—who had no belay man. Smitty made his displeasure over the idea known to the right people, and we got our slicks back immediately.

If our higher-ups had become complacent with the lack of recent major enemy activity, a VC 82-millimeter mortar attack on the Freedom Hill area and a simultaneous NVA 122-millimeter rocket attack on Da Nang Air Base one evening served as a wakeup call. The 82-millimeter stuff was for the most part poorly aimed and relatively ineffective—a few damaged buildings and minor wounds to a small number of personnel. The hit on the air base had obviously been well planned and conducted by pros. A number of aircraft in the open were destroyed, and personnel were killed. Most tragically, a direct hit on an enlisted barracks had instantly killed 133 airmen. Our location at Camp Reasoner three and a half miles away provided a nearly unobstructed vantage point for observing the hell being waged on the Air Force. The gut-wrenching *crunch* of the impacting rockets and the immense fireballs and secondary detonations were awe inspiring. As for our recon platoon, these attacks had been a first exposure to indirect fire for most of our members. For those who hadn't yet seen the light, they became instant believers that terrifying evening. Truth be told, the episode had also commanded my undivided attention.

The months flew by in a succession of boring missions and an occasional Eagle Flight. For the most part, the only tangible gains were the rapidly accumulating helicopter assaults, which counted toward another Air Medal. Before I'd realized it, I was getting short in-country. Da Nang Air Base had an excellent Chinese restaurant called the Bamboo Cottage, and in an act of mischief with my recon platoon buddies, we removed the wooden title letters from the building's front. I still have the wonton-style "B."

My twenty-fourth birthday—the second and last in Vietnam—came and went with zero fanfare. Gary sent a birthday card with the latest picture of my niece, and Mom sent a card with a snapshot of her and our little puppy, Tootie. Wisely, she didn't utter a word concerning Al or Tim. Not that the cards went unappreciated, but I admittedly felt shortchanged over not having a female squeeze sending me lewd pictures and promises of XXX-rated treatment upon my return to the World.

The NVA's 1972 Easter Offensive had begun in earnest shortly following my birthday with their major assault on an area about ninety miles north of Saigon named Loc Ninh. Literally overnight, the lethargic attitude prevalent in the brigade transformed to one of hyper-alertness. Charlie Ridge, literally right up the street from Camp Reasoner, had been a major enemy staging area since the Marines had owned it, and the gooks were most likely gathering their ducks to hit us also along with the air base and Da Nang proper.

The platoon had been conducting a local sweep mission at the bottom southwest finger of Charlie Ridge when I spotted a VC soldier standing atop a large boulder about 250 meters distant. Armed with an AK-47 casually draping from his neck sling, he resembled more a tourist taking in the sights than an OP scanning for Americans. Unbelievably, he hadn't seen us. I beckoned Bones to my side, drew a bead, and squeezed the trigger. The gook jerked abruptly and cart-wheeled down the right face of the boulder as if in a Hollywood stunt. Excitedly glancing to my left, I remarked to Bones that we could chalk off another gook sent to Buddha when I noticed his pained grimace. His eardrums had taken a hit from the muzzle blast.

Smitty called in the contact report to battalion and was instructed to develop the situation. Proceeding toward the position where I dropped the gook, we received incoming with telltale green tracers from an RPD light machine gun, the Chicom-Soviet equivalent to our own M-60. The RPD was a weapon that truly commanded one's attention, and along with the rest of the crew, I thought it prudent to silence the thing as soon as possible. I had never had the opportunity to fire a live round from an M-72 LAW, much less use one on the gooks. Seizing this golden and probably last opportunity, I commandeered PFC Joe Romero's LAW and aimed the thing where I guessed the RPD to be. A nice orange fireball and ugly black smoke appeared—no more noise from the RPD.

Following a brief period of silence, the gooks began probing us with sporadic AK-47 fire from our distant right front. This was a common trick employed by the NVA—dupe your opponent into believing they'd encountered a pushover force of ragbags, then hammer them when they'd taken the bait. Colonel Negris showed up on the scene in his Huey, and although he'd meant well, the noise from the thing wasn't helping us one iota for estimating enemy strength and localizing their position.

A pair of Cobra gunships soon arrived on station and immediately received heavy light-weapons fire. The lead ship reported seventy to eighty heavily armed gooks in the open

approximately 300 meters from our location, which Smitty
knew to be way over our heads for a contest. As a result, Lieutenant Colonel Negris ordered our element out of the area for
a foot return to Camp Reasoner. Along with the Cobras, a
company from our neighboring 1st Battalion, 46th Infantry,
would clean up the gooks.

Back at Reasoner later that afternoon, we received word
that the line company had inflicted sixty-five confirmed enemy
KIAs, with no friendly casualties. Most importantly, they'd captured highly detailed NVA attack plans for taking out the
entire Da Nang tactical area. Like most of the platoon, I felt
slighted for having been kicked out of the party, but we all
realized that it could very well have been the last one in this
life. Hell, maybe the recon platoon had even averted a real
massacre on the good guys.

The platoon's second and final casualty during my time
with them occurred around mid-May during an operation in
the Quang Ngai area. The place was the usual dense-as-hell
highland rain forest—right out of the *Jungle Book*—and was yet
another popular hangout for gooks infiltrating from the
north. We'd been ascending a grueling 500-meter terrain feature when Bones, on point with me as slack, encountered a
lone NVA soldier armed with an AK. The gook tagged two
rounds in Bones's stomach before he could react, and I
dropped the gook with a double-tap to his brain as he turned
to run. The guy had literally come out of nowhere, and I knew
that he had to have company farther up the hill or maybe even
had additional buddies trailing us. Having recovered my wits
and with Bones screaming in pain, I yelled for Doc Boyden to
get working on him while Smitty called Reasoner for an emergency extraction and gunship support. Dave meanwhile
posted LP/OPs about fifty meters to our front, rear, and flanks
as a stopgap measure against further surprises.

We hadn't as yet encountered further contact, and Doc
advised Smitty that we had to get Bones down the hill to a
pickup area as soon as possible. To my question of how badly
Bones was hit, Doc replied that he didn't believe the slugs had

hit any vital areas, but he was concerned over possible internal bleeding. He hoped that the main source of the pain was being caused by spasmodic stomach muscles. I instructed SP4 Chris Conlin and PFC Dave Hiner to pack Bones in a makeshift poncho-liner litter, with PFC Jerry Fields holding an IV, and the platoon cautiously reversed course back down the hill.

Two AH1-G Huey Cobra gunships arrived on station in advance of our extraction choppers, and from what we could hear over the frequency and the detonations taking place on the hilltop, they'd found somebody for sure, which turned out to be an NVA battalion command post with a reinforced rifle company for security. Two F-4 Phantoms from Da Nang Air Base showed up and really started giving the creeps a good hosing down with Vulcan cannons and bombs. If we hadn't ran into the gook, who was no doubt a trail watcher, his partners uphill would most likely have mauled us before help arrived. Dumb luck.

Soon landing back at Camp Reasoner, I made a beeline for the brigade dispensary where the medics had taken Bones for initial treatment. As it happened, I'd stepped into the ward just in time to witness our battalion commander, Lt. Col. Rocco Negris, award Bones his second Purple Heart. Captain Steele, Top Yeast, Smitty, and Dave were also on hand to provide their support. When I finally had Bones alone, he grabbed my hand in a grimace. For a split second, my mind flashed back to that depressing day in the 24th Evacuation ICU ward years ago when I'd visited John Gentile. Bones lived to tell the story and was soon medevac'd to Japan and finally to Womack Army Hospital at Fort Bragg. (We'd soon link up again back in the World.)

With the NVA's Easter Offensive gaining ever more momentum, the small ville of Tan An Phuong, located about two klicks west-southwest of Charlie Ridge, also became a primary concern of infiltration. Granted, the gooks had for the most part been avoiding major contacts with friendly units, mainly just waiting for us to get the hell out of Dodge and jump on our freedom birds, but the fact that they were out there was reason enough to be in alert mode. During a night-long probe mission on foot, I gave the area a once-over with the Starlight scope, which yielded only a dog about 250 meters distant pulling "guard duty." The dog naturally alerted as we inched closer to the ville, and rather than shooting, a gook yelled through a bullhorn, "Go home, GIs! The war is over for you! Do you really want to die now with being so close to leaving our country?" The gook spoke fluent English with virtually no accent, which really got our attention. The scene reminded me of the movie *Pork Chop Hill* when the enemy yelled through a PA system at Gregory Peck's company. All that was missing were the floodlights. Smitty saw no future in stirring up shit, nor did Lieutenant Colonel Negris back at Reasoner, and we disengaged for home.

Later on back at Reasoner, Smitty, Dave, and I discussed the evening's activities. Dave's and my desires had been to tangle with the gooks, but Smitty's reality check set us straight. There must have been plenty of gooks out there, and the manner in which they'd literally spared our lives was ample proof that they weren't intimidated by a puny American recon element. Many of the brigade's line units had already stood down and had their manpower shipped back to the World. Were a major battle to erupt, we probably wouldn't stand a Chinaman's chance, at least from a troop-strength standpoint. Better to live and let live for a change.

My very last mission in-country was securing FSB Linda's dismantling. Late that evening, I developed a stomach virus that had me bent over in agony and bowing to puke most of the night. It was raining cats and dogs, and I slept fitfully in a semicomatose condition, thanks to whatever pills Doc Boyden provided, under a large cardboard sheet. As bad as I felt, if we'd been hit, I'd most likely have told the gooks to just finish me off.

A bright day dawned with my guts restored to seminormalcy and my time with the platoon ended. Smitty informed the Huey crew who was to fly me back to Camp Reasoner that I'd be leaving country the following day, and I was given the

DEROS ride of a lifetime. As soon as the bird had cleared the hilltop, the aircraft commander pitched the nose straight down and hugged the hillside like a diving predator to the valley floor far below. As a further gesture of respect, the crew chief tossed out several M-18 smoke canisters in a final pyrotechnic display of congratulations and farewell. Meanwhile, I relished a final mad minute by expending my M-16 ammo on the hostile enemy vegetation. I'd just completed my tour with the last infantry ground-maneuver unit in-country, and all of our folks would follow me home twenty-four days later.

During final out-processing later that afternoon, I was presented a second Air Medal and a second ARCOM. Big goddamned deal, I thought. I was still highly agitated over having been denied the in-country extension and felt as if I had nothing worthwhile to return home to. The best description would probably be my sense of having become an angry and empty shell, basically dead with a life ended at age twenty-four.

I departed Da Nang Air Base for the final time on June 5, 1972, with orders for the 82nd Airborne Division, having spent an additional nine months living in the jungle with the platoon. I left behind good buddies such as Smitty, Dave Smith, Bones Hall, Doc Boyden, Henry Arocha, and Chris Conlin. As the World Airways DC-8 leveled at cruise altitude, I gazed out the window at the receding Vietnamese coastline. When it was no longer visible, I briefly asked myself if I'd remember this place and the things I'd seen and done years or even decades hence. I knew the answer all too well. I fell into a restless sleep, clueless that I'd again set foot here slightly less than twenty-nine years later.

I called Mom at work during our refueling stop in Anchorage to inform her of our landing at Travis within the next few hours. We hadn't been checked at Da Nang Air Base for contraband, and I experienced a bout of near-panic upon learning we'd be processed through U.S. Customs in the Travis MAC arrival area. Dad's Walther P-38 gift was hidden between my legs, supported only by my skivvies (it actually worked pretty well), and I prayed that the agents weren't conducting frisks or employing a metal detector. Just what Mom would need—witnessing her son being hauled off to jail by the APs on a federal weapons rap. The agent gave my kit bag a cursory pat-down, and there stood Mom smiling at the nearby exit door. The reunion was joyous, but she'd been somewhat shaken up by the large group of war protesters standing vigil outside the gate.

Through bitter past experience, I'd long ago figured out that a grateful welcoming parade wouldn't be in the cards during my final homecoming, but the counterculture always had something new in store for GIs. And Mom hadn't understated what awaited us for a greeting party. My instincts held true as we approached the base's exit gate, and I locked onto a freak who was yelling at his cohorts and pointing at me. I saw a large tomato in his right hand. To his credit, he had an arm like Don Drysdale and nearly shattered the front passenger door window. My first inclination was to have Mom jam on the brakes so I could leap out and deck him, backup buddies or not. By now, Mom was totally panicked, and when we'd attained out-of-range distance from the crowd I soothingly told her pull over—I'd drive us home. Here I was back in the states barely thirty minutes, and I'd been attacked by my own countrymen. Welcome back to the World.

My old Special Forces classmate Sgt. Dane M. (Mark) "Combat" Kelly and I had become inseparable buddies in the 196th, and through good fortune, we DEROS'd two days apart. We linked up at my home in Manteca, and for the next thirty days, we raised hell in Manteca and his home in Granite Falls, Washington. Together, we obtained our basic and advanced scuba-diver ratings with Everett Skindivers in Everett, Washington. Managing to secure the same assignments with a recon platoon in the 82nd Airborne at Fort Bragg, we promptly became known as the Bobsey Twins.

Epilogue

A succession of postings followed my service in Vietnam over the next four and a half years, beginning with a fourteen-month stint in a recon platoon with HHC, 2nd Battalion, 504th Infantry, at Fort Bragg. A highlight was the the platoon was the first military unit to navigate North Carolina's Cape Fear River from Fort Bragg to Wilmington Bay in RB-15 boats over a five-day period. Upon arriving in Wilmington, the city council honored us with a barbecue and invitated us to spend the night on the decks of the retired battleship *North Carolina*.

Assignments with Company B (Ranger), 75th Infantry, and Company B, 3rd Battalion, 47th Infantry, at Fort Lewis and as a training NCO in a basic-combat-training unit at Fort Ord followed, culminating in recon assistant platoon sergeant duties with Combat Support Company, 2nd Battalion, 32nd Infantry, also at Fort Ord.

I also served special duty with the Fort Ord pistol team. Using match-grade M-1911 and .22 High Standard pistols in "combat" and "leg" competitions against other 6th Army Marksmanship Team hopefuls, I barely missed the cut for the 6th Army's team and the national matches at Camp Perry, Ohio. Still, it wasn't a bad showing for an "off the rack" neophyte with no background in competitive marksmanship.

Since I held senior scuba diver certification, I was tasked with directing swimmer screening for the platoon's attendance at the U.S. Marine Corps Amphibious Reconnaissance Course at Coronado Naval Base in San Diego. Once again, I was privileged to participate in an historical event: we were the first intact other-service unit to undergo the arduous two-week

213

training program conducted on Red Beach and in San Diego Bay—a spirit-boosting finale to my active army service.

With my expiration, term of service (ETS), rapidly approaching in September 1976, I faced the choice of remaining on active duty for a command-sponsored tour with the Berlin Brigade (not on my career wish list) or duty exemption for the "Project Transition" program. After much soul-searching, I chose to finish my FAA private pilot certificate training at Del Monte Aviation in Monterey, California, of which I had completed about half in 1968–69 and which was a prerequisite for advanced pilot training on the GI Bill. The army held me thirty days past ETS for transfer to the medical retired list, and I passed the check ride with aviation legend Bob Brown on October 15, 1976. I signed out of the unit two days later on terminal leave, with an effective retirement date of December 7, 1976.

Many events, good and otherwise, occurred during my active service to Uncle Sam. The years since have also had their ups and downs, for both myself and our country. I'm a veteran of four marriages and pretty much restrict my personal contacts to fellow vets and a very few trusted civilian friends. As for our great country, it's been devastating to observe the tragic and relentless erosion of our traditional morals, values, and patriotism.

At the beginning of the Gulf War during early 1991, our N/75 Ranger company medic, Mike "Doc" Creamer, ravaged by survivor guilt and despondent over the problems plaguing our country, chose to end his life. Trust me, Mike was a man's man, and for him to do so was an ultimate act of not only desperation, but outright defiance of a system gone awry.

Urged on by Gary Linderer, I attended my first ever military reunion during 2000 at Fort Campbell, Kentucky. My mind was in a literal spin upon being reunited with fellow F/58 LRPs I hadn't seen or spoken to in over thirty-three years.

While sharing the honored company of twelve fellow combat veterans, I returned to Vietnam for three weeks in early 2001. Sponsored by the nonprofit organization "Vietnam, a

Quest for Healing" and led by the program's director, Sgt. 1st Class Walter "Waldo" Bacak, a fellow LRRP/Ranger and loyal friend who served heroically as our mother and confidante, the trip amounted to what I can best describe as a love-hate experience. Inevitably, some of the population treated us with disdain. Unexpectedly, most were friendly and giving. In one aspect, I consider myself fortunate in having been chosen for such a once-in-a-lifetime experience. But in another, I have yet to sort the whole thing out. Maybe I never will.

Soon after the Vietnam trip I received a phone call from a long lost twangy voice: "My name is Ranger Roger Brown, and are you the same Dave Walker I knew in F/58 LRP and N/75 Ranger?" And that's how the long-broken circle was reclosed. Since that fateful conversation, I've attended four reunions of the 75th Ranger Regiment Association at Columbus, Georgia. Retired Capt. "Hog" Brown and his lovely wife, Rangerette Linda, hold a biennial beerfest and barbecue for his 101st and 173rd LRRP-LRP-Ranger boys on their vast ranch in Upatoi, Georgia; it would make Ted Turner envious. Most uplifting— and an outright honor—was a 2004 request from Reed Cundiff, our 173rd LRRP-LRP-Ranger Unit Director, that I assist in assembling the nomination packet for Roger's 2005 induction into the U.S. Army Ranger Hall of Fame at Fort Benning, Georgia. This vital mission was executed as planned at Benning's Infantry Hall, and I remain most humbled and proud to have served not only with Ranger Brown, but other such noteworthy warriors.

Should I ever be called upon once again to defend our at-present mortally endangered country, I'll do so with the unqualified patriotism and zeal of that innocent seventeen-year-old kid I knew decades ago. And should I cash in the chips, what more befitting and greater fate for a warrior? Any still-stuck-in-the-60s flower children out there with contrary thoughts are formally invited to meet me in the alley of their choosing, but I doubt there'll be any takers once they've looked in a mirror and finally seen what they really are.

Long-Range Patrol

Lurking amidst the jungle gloom, knowing not whether the next Sunrise shall greet us with His warm, reassuring rays, a sense of foreboding prevails amongst Us Six.

The snap of a twig; an abrupt silence; a disturbance in the triple-canopy rain forest enveloping us—all can, and have, spelled instantaneous oblivion for others of our unforgiving and deadly profession.

Vigilance, proficiency, and indeed, luck, are our keys to survival in this all-encompassing, hostile environment.

For there is no quarter in this game.

The atmosphere is electrified with His presence.

Our eyes and ears are as one, every sense keenly attuned, searching for, listening to, analyzing that which is not of ours or Nature's.

For He is out there; by no timetable must He abide, watching for, awaiting, anticipating our fatal error.

Stealth, discipline, and caution have, on this mission, proven to no avail.

Our hearts cease, minds race, as we simultaneously detect the firing device's telltale action.

A millisecond's blinding flash of light is accompanied by an ear-shattering thunder.

And then there is nothing.

We Six have embarked upon our journey through the infinite expanse of time . . .

Acknowledgments

My boundless thanks are due a number of outstanding fellow Vietnam combat veteran buddies for their unflagging input and encouragement during this book's composition. To Gary A. Linderer, who—in addition to providing the foreword for this book—prodded a brother LRP/Ranger along when things slowed to a snail's crawl, and Capt. Roger B. "Hog" Brown, my early LRP mentor, special friend, and combat savior, for his glowing preface. And to Capt. Larry Bailey, Don Bendell, Lt. Col. Gary E. Dolan, CW5 William T. "W. T." Grant, Kenn Miller, Steven L. Waterman, Maj. Jim Morris, Lt. Col. Robert K. Brown, and Maj. Mark "Zippo" Smith for their charitable endorsements. To my editors, Chris Evans and Dave Reisch, and art director Wendy Reynolds at Stackpole Books for their invaluable help and patience.

About the Author

David Paul Walker was born to George Ernest and Ardis Margaret (Milligan/Wright) Walker on April 6, 1948, in the French Hospital in San Francisco, California. Initially being raised in that city and North Hollywood, the family relocated to Hayward in the San Francisco East Bay area in 1952, finally settling in central California's San Joaquin Valley town of Manteca in 1962. Following his U.S. Army enlistment as an Infantry and Airborne volunteer in July 1965, he ultimately served nearly ten years on active duty through 1976 with Airborne, Long-Range Patrol, Ranger, and conventional Infantry units, including an assignment in Germany and multiple Vietnam tours.

At the end of 1976, Staff Sergeant Walker was (again) medically retired from active duty for combat wounds received in Vietnam during early 1968, after which he pursued advanced flight training under the GI Bill, ultimately logging more than 15,000 flight hours in an assortment of forty-two general aviation aircraft as a flight instructor, charter pilot, sheriff's air transport deputy, and overnight air-freight feeder captain through 1998. Over his long civilian flying career, Captain Walker acquired U.S. Federal Aviation Administration professional credentials for Airline Transport Pilot, Certified Flight Instructor Single/Multi-Engine/Instrument Airplane, and Ground Instructor, as well as USFS/OAS/CDF pilot and NOAA/NWS Aviation Weather Observer certifications.

He currently resides with his wife, Chris, on their eleven-acre ranch in the Sierra Nevada Mountain foothills of northern California. His military awards and decorations include the Combat Infantry Badge 1st Award; Master Parachutist Badge;

Bronze Star; Purple Heart; Air Medal with "2" device; Army Commendation Medal with one oak leaf cluster; Good Conduct Medal 2nd Award; Jungle Expert Brand; 101st Recondo Brand; Expert Badge with rifle, pistol, and machine-gun bars; Vietnam Army Parachutist Badge (basic); Vietnam Service Medal with one silver and two bronze campaign stars; and Vietnam Campaign Medal with "60" device.

AFFILIATIONS
75th Ranger Regiment Association (Life Member)
Silver Wings Fraternity
101st Airborne Division LRRP-Ranger Association
Military Order of the Purple Heart
Veterans of Foreign Wars (Life Member)
SSI (formerly NASDS) Advanced SCUBA Diver
U.S. Parachute Association
Combat Infantrymen's Association
U.S Army Ranger Association (Life Member)

Stackpole Military History Series

Real battles. Real soldiers. Real stories.

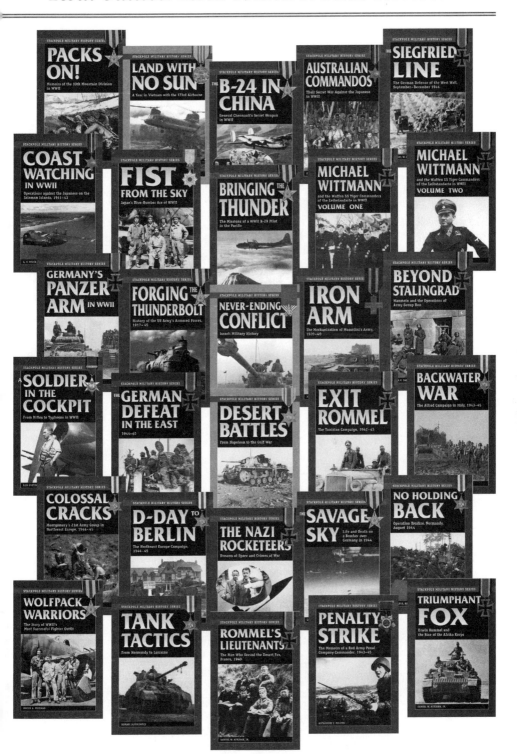

Stackpole Military History Series

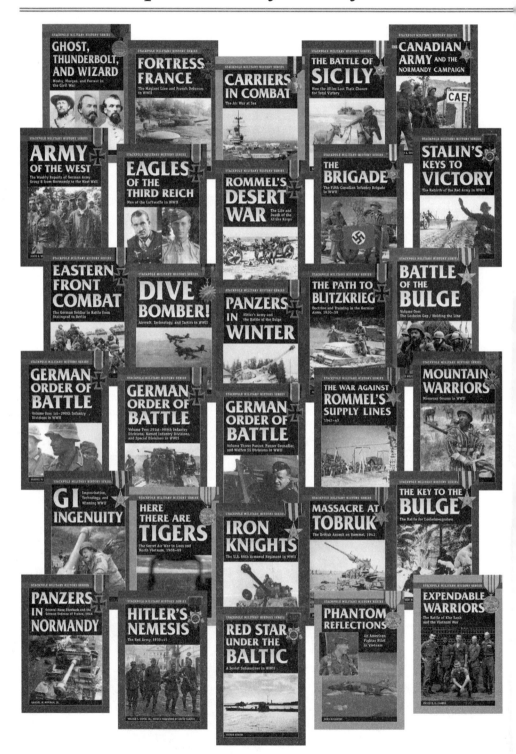

Real battles. Real soldiers. Real stories.

Stackpole Military History Series

NEW for Fall 2010

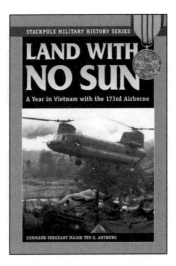

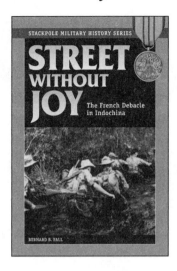

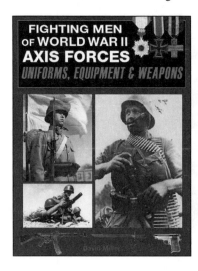
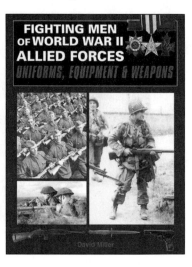